I'M JUST
A PERSON

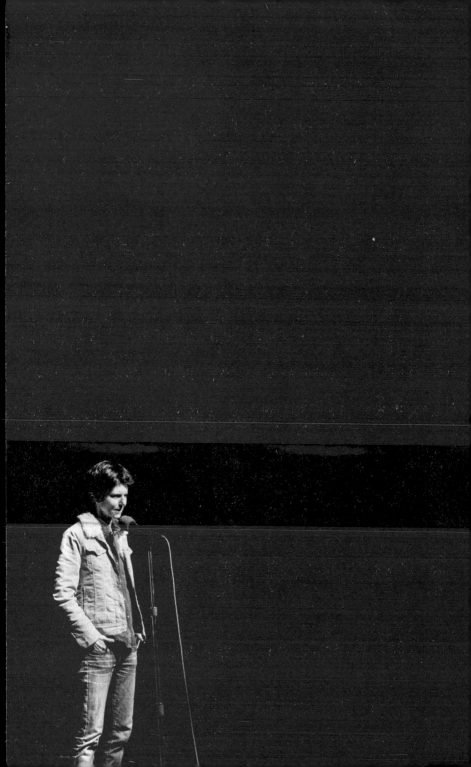

I'M JUST A PERSON

—

TIG NOTARO

ecco

An Imprint of HarperCollinsPublishers

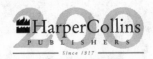
HarperCollins
PUBLISHERS
— Since 1817 —

HarperCollins books may be purchased for educational,
business, or sales promotional use. For information please e-mail
the Special Markets Department at SPsales@harpercollins.com.

A hardcover edition of this book was published in 2016 by Ecco,
an imprint of HarperCollins Publishers.

FIRST ECCO PAPERBACK EDITION PUBLISHED 2017.

Designed by Ashley Tucker
Illustrations by Tony Achilles

Library of Congress Cataloging-in-Publication Data
has been applied for.

ISBN 978-0-06-226664-4

17 18 19 20 21   LSC   10 9 8 7 6 5 4 3 2 1

Sept. 22, 1986

This is a very pleasant moment for me. Your request has made me realize that I, as many parents have taken Tig's good qualities, treasured them — and taken them for granted.

Tig has been a delightful child. Her personality has captured the hearts of our family and friends. She is and has always been very creative. Tig uses her hands with dexterity and has skillfully made things with wisdom and thought of the individual.

Tig has a very keen sense of humor.

Tig is and has always been very well coordinated.

Tig is an extremely sensitive girl and truthful to a fault!

She is a creative girl but a realistic young adult.

Tig cares a great deal about the welfare of people or animals — She is a unique young person —

I love her.

Susie Cusack

Dear Tig

Glad we got a chance to talk. If there is anything additional that you ever want to share, I certainly would welcome the opportunity to visit with you either on the phone or in person.

I hardly see your move as making you a "drifter", partner. Some people could sit in a house, the same house for years and be adrift, with no goals no ambition, letting talent rot.

Keep on being creative, as _you_ see fit and don't listen to any-damn-body. All my life I wished I could sing. I barely have been able to howl at the full moon. Your consistent pursuit of music is a source of pride and I tell many people of your talents. Do what you want to do; do what you gotta do.

After you get settled, and feel better about getting around, let me know and I'll arrange a visit out there. Hopefully we will have time and resources to see my mother.

Mom's situation is a constant source of revelation. Frances said they discontinued one of mom's meds, and she got better. Go figure. I talked to a physician, the doctor that did surgery on me twice, about this ethical situation of mother's illness. Dr. Zork is a modern Catholic, but has been a Catholic longer than he has been a doctor. He still says

the merciful thing to do is NOT USE A
feeding tube. She has STATED she chooses
to meet her MAKER, without the drawn-out
Agony And humiliation she might even be being
subjected to now. HE says that the feeding
tube type of THERAPY is to ASSIST IN the
resumption of A normal life. THAT APPARENTLY
is NOT mothers CASE, NOR will it be.

Speaking of doctors And hospitals I must again
tell you how grateful I Am for the phone
calls And letters this time LAST YEAR, when
I was in the hospital. I have REGRETTED
MANY times NOT being closer to you, even
if it meant mowing yards for A job, to live
close by. My MIND is NO longer clouded As it
was for so MANY YEARS, And these THREE
past years HAVE BEEN the basis of A foundation
for what MAY be A wonderful future. Today
that includes you, ON WHATEVER basis And
form it TAKES. Having A CLEAR HEAD mostly
yields CLEAR thoughts And plans.

I was so PLEASANTLY surprised to hear from
you when I was ill, I still feel so
lucky to still be Able to communicate
with you.

LET me know if this is A workAble Address,
by giving me A quick CALL. I say quick call
because, it will have to be on "our dime".

You can call anytime of course, But if we
get Long winded, the economy time, After 10pm,
is significant. I work AT the Holiday Inn
Bethesda, Sun-Thursday nights.

If you feel like it, send me a tape of some thing you ARE comfortable with me hearing.

Let me hear from you when you get a chance.

I love you,

Still your Dad.

———

Acknowledgments

I always considered myself a private person—both on-stage and off—who made way more observations about the world around me than the one inside me.

But after my life fell apart in March of 2012, I felt compelled to express myself on a much deeper level. With each new project I took on, I found a sense of openness, a desire to share another level of my life, and I felt a more complete person emerging.

I consider my comedy album *Live*, which was recorded at Largo, to be the skeleton of who I am and what happened directly after the rug was yanked out from under me. It was the first time that I felt a need to tell the truths of my life because there was nothing left to protect. The documentary about me that soon followed, I consider my organs, and this book, I consider to be the meat of it all. I am forever grateful for all the people who allowed me the opportunity to tell my story in all its different forms and forums.

My hope is that this book might give you some courage, and possibly some insight or understanding about me, but more ideally, about yourself. I'd be honored if someone could use my life as an example in some way, but please remember, I'm just a person. I was fumbling and failing, growing and changing through it all and will continue to do so. I tell myself daily that we all have tailbones; that though our bodies have evolved to the point of no longer needing them, our tails once gave us balance as we walked; that I'm just simply a person with a tailbone making my way in the world.

I want to thank my first hero, my mother, Susie, for giving me every single one of my talents as an athlete, artist, and comedian as well as an inner core of steel; my father, Pat, for giving me my gumption; my stepfather, Ric, for giving me the guidance that allowed me to focus that talent and gumption; my brother, Renaud, for doing anything in the world for me . . . and I mean ANYTHING (I'd do the same for you); and my manager, Hunter Seidman, who has helped me juggle these difficult times and whose keen judgments have always made everything easier and better for me.

I am deeply grateful to my agents, Andrew Skikne, Kate Edmonds, and Marc Gerald; my attorney, Julian

Zajfen; and everyone at HarperCollins and Ecco, especially Hilary Redmon, Daniel Halpern, and Gabriella Doob for their editorial insights. To the brilliant Stef Willen, who ripped this book apart a million times over to help make it what it is today. To my friends and family, all the way from Mississippi to Louisiana to Texas to Ohio to New Jersey to New York to Colorado to California and beyond—I couldn't be surrounded by more interesting, giving, open, or understanding people, so thank you.

Finally, endless gratitude to Stephanie Notaro, my tremendous wife and the adoring mother of our little kitty, Fluff, . . . every single morning that we wake up, I still can't believe the easy love we have found in each other. I am in absolute and utter awe of your tasteful ways and inspired by the high roads you take. There isn't a wiser, kinder, more hilarious, more compassionate, or more beautiful person out there. Thank you for loving me.

I'M JUST
A PERSON

1

Over My Mother's Dead Body

I don't like small talk.

"You from around here?"

"Chilly out tonight, huh?"

So I rarely talk to strangers, especially cabbies. I'll usually put my headphones on to avoid such moments.

Tonight, though, I really needed to connect with someone, anyone. And up drove anyone.

"Hi," I said softly as I got into the cab. All I could see of the driver was the profile of a man in his late forties. "Could you take me to the northwest area of Houston, please?"

"What's the address?" he sneered, disgusted that I'd been so casual, so sure that he had the kind of time to just start driving me in a general direction.

"I can't remember exactly, but if you drive me to the Spring area, I'll figure out where I'm going."

I was a shell of a human. I had just been released from one hospital for a bacterial infection and was trying to leave another hospital. This time, though, I was leaving my dead mother behind. It felt completely wrong, but what could I do? Ask the cabdriver if I could bring her with me?

*Hey, Cabby—I do understand that I'm the one
with the bad attitude, but not only do I need a
second to shut my door before you peel out of here,
but could you give me a minute to go grab my dead
mother's body?*

It was 3 A.M., and I had been at my mother's bedside for twelve hours. I was exhausted, but now that I was leaving I felt like there'd been some kind of permanent exchange. I took my sadness and left a body.

Maybe I was expecting the nurses, administrators, and doctors to gather around my mother and reminisce:

Oh, remember when she first got wheeled in here?

*Oh yeah . . . I forgot about that. I was
remembering that time when the priest came in to
read her her last rites.*

What about when we took her off life support?

Right! Yeah—she was so great. I really liked her.

My mother had died two hours before. There was no "last breath," only her death rattle—the eerie gurgling and drowning noise in her throat ending with a dark gray liquid pouring out of her mouth and dripping down her chin and neck. I sometimes wonder what my mother would think about me revealing such intimate details about her death. But my mother didn't like to edit me. When she did, all I had to say was "But it's the truth," and she'd shrug her shoulders like "Who could argue with that?"

When I called the house to tell my brother, Renaud, and stepfather, Ric, that my mother had died, Renaud said he was coming to get me. The hospital was forty-five minutes away.

An hour passed. I called my brother's phone and found out that he hadn't left the house yet. He was calling friends and family to tell them about my mother. How could this not wait? He surely didn't have an easy night, but I know he hadn't spent the last twelve hours at our mother's side counting the seconds between her breaths. I could hear in his voice how sorry he was and how much he realized he had screwed up, but I was furious, so I just took a taxi. Maybe this was a clear example of when I could have been better at picking my battles since I could not even remember my mother's address.

The cabdriver turned and stared at me for a couple beats, then cocked his head to the side and said, "You don't know the address? You don't know the address?! I need the *exact* address!"

This was not the anyone I would be opening up to. I wasn't going to the house I grew up in. Ric and my mother had moved about five years ago. My relationship with them was complicated, and I had only visited maybe five times.

"Please, I don't know it off the top of my head and my mother just died. And . . ." I started crying.

"Oh!" The cabdriver fully turned his body toward me. "'My mother just died?! My mother just died!!' Poor you!" He was yelling, his eyes bulging and squinting. "My mom left me when I was fifteen years old! She didn't give a shit about me! At least you had a mom!"

I realized this man was most likely on crack or meth and was capable of hurting me. I went quiet, asking him to please take me to the side of town I needed to go to. He began driving quickly and recklessly, periodically turning around to yell about some brutality he'd suffered in his bad life and then slam me with a final "So, you think YOU have it bad?!" I didn't care. I didn't care if our car crashed. I didn't care about anything. I just told him I was sorry. I was utterly defeated and numb. I was outside of my body, watching myself travel away from the hospital, away from watching my mother die, away from that part of my life forever.

We were getting close to the house when we took an odd exit on the freeway and pulled up to a convenience store. A completely different, and seemingly caring, cabdriver turned around to ask, "You want anything?" Mainly what I wanted was for him not to murder me at a Quickie Mart. This madman's sudden attempt at kindness wasn't any less disturbing than his unpredictable rage. It seemed somehow so disrespectful to my mother that I was even in this situation, discussing her demise with this lowlife.

"No, thank you," I said quietly and politely. Even though I couldn't really ingest food, I did want a last meal if I was about to be raped and murdered, but I didn't want it from a convenience store shelf. I guess, if I'm honest, I do feel above that. I watched him go inside and walk around, and became pretty convinced that he was just combing the aisles for a bright orange extension cord to tie my scrawny limbs together in order to get the job done. Even when he came back with snacks, I was still certain something horrible was about to happen. I mean, why else on earth did he have to stop for pink Hostess Sno Balls right then?

Was I even in the right life anymore? My mother had died two hours ago. I'd lost so much weight, my pants were falling off. I was waiting for my murderer/rapist to purchase artificial sponge cake.

When our taxi pulled back onto the freeway and headed in the right direction, I let myself be a little relieved that my life wasn't going to end behind a Quickie Mart. Or at least not tonight.

We pulled up to my mother's house, I earnestly thanked him for the ride—for not killing me, really—and he earnestly said he was sorry about my mother. He had calmed down even more and was a completely different man from the one who had picked me up. He could even pass as normal. But just in case, I tipped him well so he wouldn't come back and murder me and what was left of my family.

My brother and Ric greeted me with awkward man hugs and "I love you's." I returned the hugs and the "I love you's" probably just as manly and awkwardly. I was in a daze. Every other time in my life that I'd come home at this hour, Ric and Renaud had been in bed, and my mother had surfaced from her room to greet me.

"Hi, Sugah, you have fun?" she'd say in her thick New Orleans accent, squinting at me in the hall light in her slip.

The family cat, Bunny, popped her head up from the other side of the couch and stared at the three of us. I had given Bunny to my mother and Ric when I started touring as a stand-up full time. My mother adored Bunny. She constantly brushed her long black fur and bought her new toys, and Bunny, who was elderly, weakly batted at whatever new thing was placed in front of her and then quickly fell back asleep as if nothing had happened. Bunny was the only living thing in our house that didn't know something was terribly wrong tonight. Then again, she didn't know my mother's name. She didn't know her own name. She didn't know she was a cat. She didn't know she lived in Spring, Texas. She didn't know there was such a thing as the outdoors. Or the indoors, for that matter. She is an uninformed hairball. Even on this horrible night, she would soon be back asleep, once she found an ever-so-slightly-better position. I didn't feel as though I'd ever be able to find an ever-so-slightly-better position again. I was a stranger to myself.

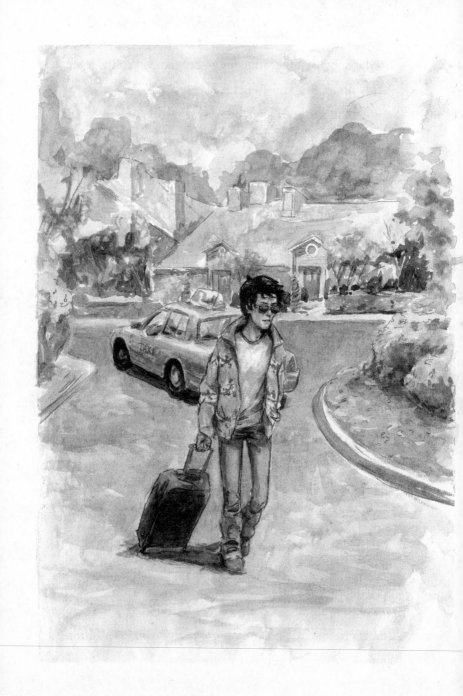

I walked down the hall toward my bedroom past a long table full of framed family photos.

Hi, Sugah, you have fun?

Not tonight, you died.

My mother was an artist, and my bedroom wall was covered with her paintings. The odd thing was, my mother was so imaginative, but her subjects seemed so everyday: portraits, trees, fall leaves, and mountain scenes. I think most of her art stemmed from her simple love of nature. Anywhere I went in my life, she wanted to know, "Oh, Sweetie, how do the trees look?" I grew up hearing, "Tig! Wow! Come here and look at this squirrel out the window. Isn't he adorable?" as if, somehow, a koala bear had found its way into our suburban Texas tree. She'd leave food out for the armadillos, like they were beautiful hummingbirds and not large, hard-shelled Texas rats, and she'd lovingly check on frogs that lived in her outdoor potted plants. Her Polaroid camera was always nearby, and she took photos of every critter that wandered or fluttered into the yard. The sky, trees, and clouds were always "magnificent!" It was like every day she was a blind person who had suddenly regained her sight.

What I thought about, lying in bed, was how I hadn't told her I was in the hospital for *Clostridium difficile*, a life-threatening bacterial infection. If I had made that one phone call, perhaps her getting up to answer the phone would have changed everything. She might have been by my side in the hospital in Los Angeles and not sitting with Ric watching late-night TV that night. She might not have gotten up when she did or nicked her leg on the end table and she wouldn't have fallen back and hit her head on the hard tile floor. Ric wouldn't have had to check her head to see if she was okay and they wouldn't have decided she was okay, and she wouldn't have stayed up to finish watching *Jimmy Kimmel Live* after Ric went to bed and Ric wouldn't have found her the next morning, still sitting up in her chair, alive but unconscious and bleeding from the nose and mouth.

I wanted to be able to picture my mother looking out of the window, saying good night to all her little friends, or asking me to get her nightly glass of ice water and put it at her bedside, but all that ran through my head that night after the taxi dropped me off was the same thing that ran through my head the night before: what I imagined to be the sound of her head hitting the floor.

2

Are You My Mother?

My mother's name was Susie, and she was raised in a sprawling home in the picturesque southern coastal town of Pass Christian, Mississippi. Her yard ended at the sands of the beach. She had horses and live-in maids, and for all the years between birth and college, she believed that water just ran through houses for free. She came from old money, and her great-grandfather had been the mayor of New Orleans. She was expected to be prim and proper, to be sweet and look beautiful. She *was* sweet and beautiful, but also wild and fearless. She was taught to ride English style, but I've heard stories about her running up from behind her horse and hopping on it bareback—behavior that her strict and controlling mother certainly didn't approve of.

Both of my parents briefly attended the University

of Southern Mississippi in Hattiesburg. My mother lived with her brother, Billy, who was friends with my father, Pat. The first time my father got a glimpse of my mother, he was walking up to their house just off campus and saw her through the window, standing at her easel painting. He said that her arms and body were just moving wildly, her brush hitting the canvas like she was conducting an orchestra. He stood there and watched, completely enamored. My mother was an art major, and I don't know what Pat was studying, but I know he was nothing like what my grandmother had pictured for her sweet, beautiful, debutante daughter. Pat wasn't exactly from the other side of the tracks. His father was a dentist in Jackson, the biggest city in Mississippi, which is probably equal to not saying anything at all. But still, I assume his upbringing was upper middle class. My mother and Pat partied relentlessly and then dropped out of college. Pat got a job working the loading dock at Sears, and my mother, who worked for less than a month in her entire life, got a job as a receptionist in a dentist's office. Three weeks later, she announced her retirement, and shortly afterward, she married, and then shortly after that, in January of 1970, she gave birth to my brother, Renaud. Welcome to the world, pal.

On March 24, 1971, I arrived. I had a serious case of jaundice, which, looking back now, was probably a hangover from my nine-month drinking binge. Had I been a more conscious fetus, I would have wished for a twin, just to have a drinking buddy in the womb.

My mother lacked certain maternal instincts. Not only was she young, but her natural inclinations were to reject conformity and raise hell. It didn't help that she herself was probably raised more by the paid help than by her own parents. Knowing only that babies needed nutrients, my mother fed us lettuce—probably iceberg—which, apparently, we "gummed to death."

After we got a few teeth and could tear through hot dogs and shrimp étouffée, she saved time and energy by setting us up in high chairs in the backyard, feeding us all three meals at once, then hosing down our diapered bodies on the lawn and letting us run around to dry off.

Pat and my mother divorced when I was six months old, and my mother moved us back to Pass Christian, where she used the outside of our new house as her canvas—painting clowns and giraffes and donkeys for our amusement—and the inside of our new house as a private saloon for her amusement. By ages four and five, my brother and I were regular barkeeps.

But we started everything early, even swimming. My mother tossed us in our neighbors' pools to teach us to swim. I was an infant, so I don't remember our swimming lessons, but I can picture her keeping us afloat by our armpits, a cigarette dangling from her lip. I also heard about them the whole time I was growing up. "Oh, your mother!" some friend of our family would fondly, disapprovingly reminisce. "We'd be at a party and see these two little babies in a pool all by themselves, and I'd say, 'Susie!' And your mother would say, 'Oh, they're little fish. Relax.'" All I can picture is my mother walking away from that conversation while two little baby heads bobbed up and down in a pool.

Whether you were male or female, my mother thought you should be able to swim before you could walk, have a firm handshake, and be able to throw a spiral with a football. These were the arbitrary standards she held everyone to, and if you couldn't meet them, she didn't fully respect you. Other than that, my mother had no boundaries and no rules. She was bold and uninhibited, and didn't care about what anybody thought of her. Even before I knew what beauty and humor were, she was the most beautiful person I'd ever seen who had me cackling with laughter when all I had to show were

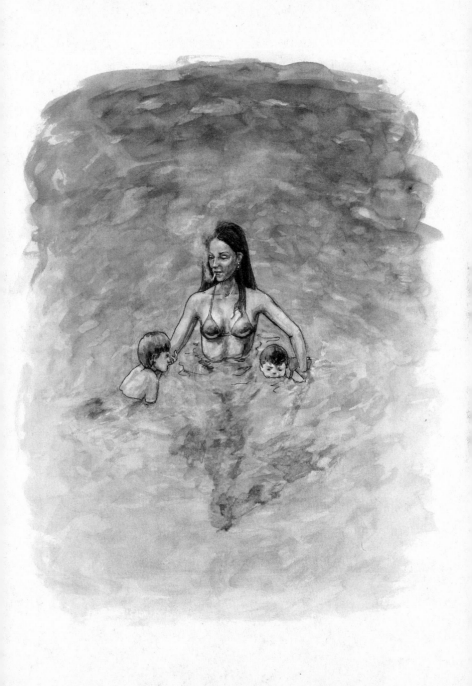

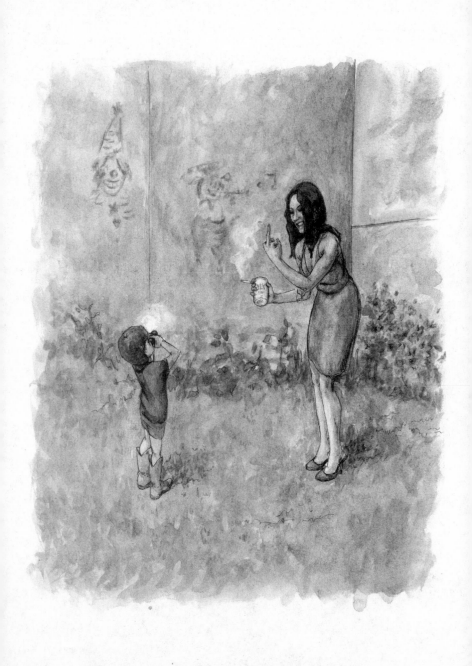

a couple of teeth. During a move in my early twenties, I seem to have permanently misplaced a photo that captures her perfectly: She's wearing a skirt, holding a beer and a cigarette in one hand, and giving the camera the middle finger with the other. I was the photographer, age six.

Because she was raised by a very uptight and judgmental mother, in a house where children were to be seen and not heard, my mother never wanted her children to feel controlled in that way. She wanted to raise us as free-spirited people who could be exactly who we wanted to be. My mother's answer to anyone who had a problem with her—or me—was "Go to hell." If someone in the grocery store cut in front of her, they could go to hell. If some kid teased me, she could go to hell. If a neighbor was upset about one of our twelve cats lounging around their pool, they could go to hell.

I was two years old when my stepfather, Ric, came along. He and my mother were set up on a blind date by my grandmother's good friend Nellie. (Of course this eighty-year-old woman's name was Nellie.) Ric checked off every box on my grandmother's suitable-husband-for-her-daughter checklist. He was an attractive, stable, kind, clean-cut attorney who had money, intelligence,

and a promising future. He quickly became a father figure, returning home from business trips bearing gifts
and regularly transforming into the Toe Monster, who
chewed on my brother's and my tiny, little, dirty Mississippi feet while we squirmed with laughter. My mother
and Ric married when I was four. A year later, Ric got a
job in Houston, and we moved to nearby Spring, Texas.

Because my mother was the type who liked to dance
on tables—at bars, weddings, parties, or any other place
she had a drink—my brother and I had developed a
shared glance of "Here we go again" at a young age.
And when Ric started traveling for business two to three
times a month, we had to look after our mother all by
ourselves. On several occasions, we woke to discover she
had snuck out after putting us to bed. My brother and I
didn't know what else to do besides call our aunt Googsie
in Mississippi. (Of course our aunt's name was Googsie.)
She managed to sound startled by the news, but in reality
was probably not the least bit surprised. Googsie tried to
reassure us that our mother would be back soon and told
us to get back in bed. For all I knew, my mother's nighttime whereabouts were the same as her daytime whereabouts: a neighbor's pool. Drinking with friends by the
pool was my mother's nine-to-five job, and she took it

very seriously. She logged an impressive number of hours poolside, many of which ended with her slamming down her beer and shooting up from a plastic chair exclaiming, "Oh, dammit, I forgot to pick up Tig!"

There were never freshly baked cookies greeting me when I came home from school, but according to my friends, I did have the "cool mom." When friends stayed for dinner, she would dye our food weird colors or take us through the drive-thru in reverse so we could order out of our passenger-side windows. When I was in sixth grade, my mother picked me and a friend up and drove us slowly home on the hood of her car. When we got to a stop sign, she pulled onto the wrong side of the road so she was next to another stopped car, leaned toward the passenger window, and yelled, "Hey, wanna drag?"

Everything was a party to my mother. Even my recreational-league soccer games. All the other parents sat on folding chairs, cheering and clapping at a reasonable volume, and my mother ran up and down the sidelines, toting a six-pack and screaming for me to "Kick the goddamn ball!" Almost every day I heard, "I wish your mom was my mom!" Stories about her always evoked "No way!" and "Your mom is unbelievable!" And sure, my mother was funny and crazy, but as unbelievable as

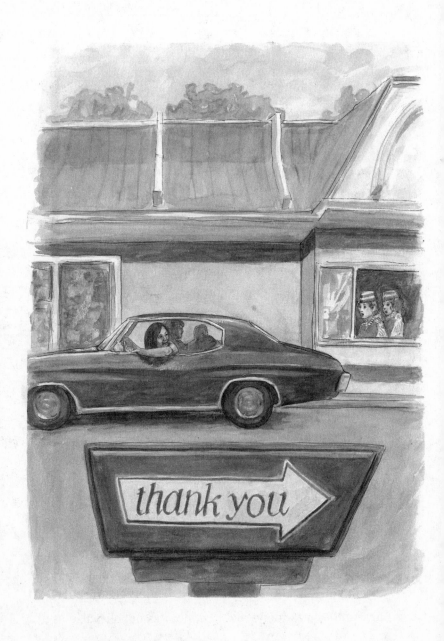

everyone thought she was, I thought that their mothers were even more unbelievable. "Wow, so you just know where your mother is at all hours?" I'd ask. Or "There's just a home-cooked meal on the table every night?" and "You don't have to go round up your mother to get her to go to bed?"

I was envious of kids with mothers who baked and did crafts and were all nosey in their business. I always tried to connect with my mother. But sometimes it seemed as though as soon as my brother and I were able to feed ourselves, my mother expected us to fend for ourselves almost entirely. We did share a sense of humor and bonded while enjoying our favorite TV shows: *All in the Family, Sanford and Son, Saturday Night Live, Late Night with David Letterman, Good Times, I Love Lucy, Laverne & Shirley,* and *Welcome Back, Kotter.* But, ultimately, I wanted to share more with my mother than a laugh together at other—made-up—families'—made-up—experiences. Sure, I had a "cool mom" who was stylish and listened to hip music at full volume, but mostly I wanted her to make me dinner and scratch my back before bed. I wanted a mother who was more likely to remember to pick me up from soccer practice than to be punctual to the neighbor's poolside happy hour or to dye the mashed potatoes blue. I wanted not to mother my mother, tracking her down so she could come home to mother me.

But I didn't have that. I had a mother I had to chase, calling around the neighborhood and telling her, "It's time to go home," or "Don't dance on the table." Ric chimed in with similar requests to "slow down" or "get off the roof." I did have some help from a few neighbors, though the neighbors adored my mother, and often explained away her pranks. My mother's good friend Lainey once had to explain to a mutual acquaintance of theirs that my mother didn't mean any real harm when she tied all her empty beer cans to this woman's rear bumper. It took a village.

My favorite thing to wear from about first to third grade was a blue T-shirt with an iron-on monkey and the caption HERE COMES TROUBLE. And that was putting it mildly. I wore that T-shirt with pride. I was trouble growing into that shirt and long past growing out of it. I didn't understand my friends and peers who lived the quiet life of the Strawberry Shortcake iron-on. To make me into the nearly perfect human being that I am today, my mother did have to discipline me. She was a very emotional disciplinarian. I guess all of her happy, crazy,

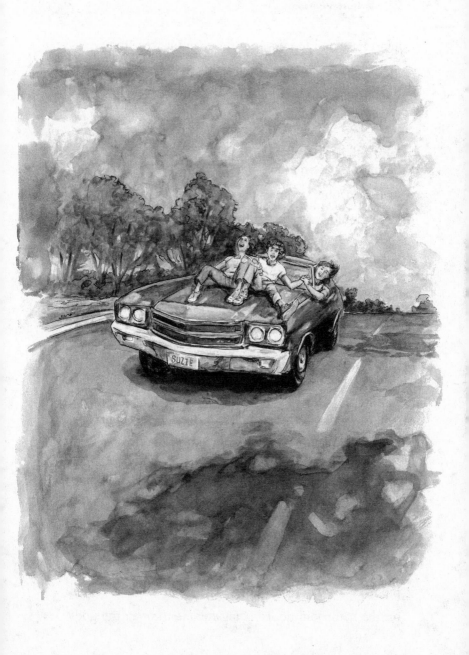

and funny had to go somewhere, and it went to crying, yelling, and slamming doors. She'd yell and slam, and then maybe thirty minutes later she'd release me from my bedroom jail cell with her teary-eyed pardon: "Sweetie, I don't want to fight." When my behavior had been really despicable, my mother typically agreed with Ric's controlled, deliberate punishments, but if I was confined to my room for too long, she always ended up missing me and would come in to sit on my bed to hug and kiss me until we made peace.

In seventh grade, I did get in a lot of trouble for smoking in our house. Ric and my mother both smoked, as did my grandparents and uncles and pretty much everyone else in our family. Yet somehow, through the thick layer of smoke that engulfed our house twenty-four hours a day, my mother smelled something from behind the closed bathroom door. Ric would have knocked once and, if I was defiant, would have wasted no time in getting a screwdriver to remove the entire door. Besides not knowing where the tools were, my mother was not somebody who could've exerted enough calm and focus to loosen a screw when her emotions were flowing. Instead, she exploded with anger, sadness, and frustration. She pounded on the bathroom door yelling for me to open the goddamn door. When I finally let her in, she took the pack and shook it in my face, asking where the hell I had gotten the cigarettes. I recall sarcastically telling her that I had to send away for them and wait six weeks. My mother had been smoking since she was a child. There are pictures of her at the age of fifteen opening presents on Christmas morning, sitting by the tree in her nightgown, a cigarette in her hand. I mean, was *that* okay? Should I have waited till Christmas?

As I got a few years older and my world expanded, I started sneaking out of the house and taking the car with me. I didn't have a license yet at age fourteen, but that didn't stop me from heading out after my mother and Ric had gone to bed and picking up friends so we could go through the twenty-four-hour drive-thrus, then cruise around smoking cigarettes, slurping milk shakes, and eating french fries all night.

I only got caught sneaking out one time. My friends Stacey and Alison and I had snagged a four-piece umbrella patio set from someone's yard and set it up in the middle of the street. We slunk back to our very strategic hiding spot, the bushes of a church—the closest I'd willingly come to the house of the Lord—and watched for cars. After an hour of crouching and peering out through the brush, watching cars swerve around stolen patio furniture every twenty minutes, we witnessed a far more sophisticated crime. Across the street, a couple of guys threw a brick through the glass door of a liquor store, backed a beater of a pickup truck up to the wreckage, hauled thousands of dollars' worth of liquor into the bed of the truck, and drove off. Clearly, God was not watching over any of us too closely since we were all committing crimes right outside his front door. But God only knows why we decided that we should be the ones to risk it all to bring justice to our community. We scrambled into my mother's car and chased the truck until we got close enough to get the license plate number, and then returned to the liquor store, where we found the owner, who had responded to his alarm system. We gave him the license plate number, feeling proud and exhilarated to be helping solve a crime, totally ignoring the fact that we'd begun our evening "borrowing" hundreds of dollars of furniture. I guess we didn't see ourselves as thieves, only clever, mischievous hell-raisers who thought they were giving locals an opportunity to see something weird. I was personally always hoping to see something weird. How could it be criminal to want to mix up the monotony on the outskirts of town?

The next morning, there wasn't a suspicious-looking

french fry in my mother's car. The gas tank may have been a quarter lower, but my mother never had a real gauge on gauges anyway. I thought I had gotten away with my nighttime nonsense as usual. Then, a few days later, my mother took me with her to run errands, making a quick stop at the liquor store. I sat in the front seat, horrified, as I watched the owner tell her a story. I slouched down, certain my sneaking-out days were about to end, especially when the owner noticed me in the car, pointed wildly, and ran out. He couldn't have been more excited to thank and hug me for helping him find robbers in the middle of the night. My mother uttered a disapproving "oh, Sweetie!" with a smirk, and seemed to be caught in the middle of being dismayed that I'd snuck out and glad, even proud, that I'd been of help.

I was also a horrible student. And my mother was at her sternest when it came to my performance in school. There was a lot of "do as I say and not as I do," since my mother hadn't done well in school or graduated from college. School had been all fun and games up until around fourth grade. I was on board with learning colors and shapes, or taking questions when the answers were chicken, duck, horse, pig, cow, goat, or sheep. But when the curriculum began to include learning to tell time or long division or memorizing the names of planets, it just wasn't fun anymore. I mean, I didn't mind easy things like "rounding off," because my answer could be "I don't know, four? Five? Get off my case, I'm rounding." Otherwise my interest level in whatever was being taught at school registered at zero.

At the end of one typically miserable school day in sixth grade, a teacher handed me a sealed envelope addressed: "To the parents of Tig Notaro." She told me not to open it. So, as I soon as I got on the bus I opened it. Inside was a form with all sorts of learning disabilities checked off that I needed to be tested for, the results of which could place me in special education. I froze and thought, "Oh my God, I'm not a genius after all." I imagined walking in the door and sitting Ric and my mother down and saying, "Dearest parents . . . I've misled you," and seeing their confused faces and reactions. That's when I'd give them the envelope and say, "Open this, it's all in here," and they'd say, "Thanks, dumbass." Then I decided that if my parents didn't know that I wasn't a genius, I didn't want to be the one to tell them. So I just hid the envelope in my closet, right next to my latent homosexuality.

Even though now I understand I probably just learned differently than some of my classmates, and that special ed might have helped me tremendously, the whole thing really did a number on my self-esteem. I assumed that if I was tested, I would qualify for special education, so I immediately accepted that I was intellectually inferior and began grading my own tests by writing an *F* at the top and then putting my head down and taking a nap while others tried to figure out the square root of this or that. As a result, I ended up in classes with all prefixes: pre, intro, informal, welcome to, not really, atta girl. If there had been a Pre PE, I would have been in it, and I wouldn't have been allowed to play, but the coach might've asked if I wanted to hold the basketball in the bleachers, you know, just to get a feel for it.

In seventh grade, just as I had done since fourth grade, I did my book report on the Beverly Cleary classic *Ribsy*—still my favorite book to this day. Apparently, I was not paying attention when the teacher gave us a list of approved books, which included *Anne Frank: The Diary of a Young Girl*, *Little Women*, and *Where the Red Fern Grows*. People my age were supposed to be reading about the horrors of the Holocaust and following plots that dealt with the certainty of death, not reading about the adventures of a skinny dog and following plots about pesky fleas.

Just to remind you, my peers were reporting on books with passages like "A quiet conscience makes one strong," and I reported on a book with sentences like "Both Joe and Ribsy were having a good time" and a chapter titled "The Cleanest Dog in the USA."

My brother was nearly a straight-A student and would go right into his room after school and do his homework, unlike me, who would usually claim that I didn't have any. And because I never planned on doing it, that was pretty much a true statement. I remember my mother always being very surprised when she heard from other parents that school projects were due. "Oh, Tig!," she might say. "You didn't tell me you had a science fair project!" I always replied with "Yeah, I already finished." It was easy to avoid being found out because she would rarely push, and if she did, I'd claim my twenty-page history report was in my locker, which, by the way, I might have trouble finding even if I had known the combination. On the rare occasion that she did push because Karen's mother said that Karen's project was almost finished and Karen's dad was helping her with it, I let my mother know my project was sitting at school with the glue drying.

The day I found out I had failed my first eighth grade, I was hanging out in my friend Michele's bedroom looking at posters of Eddie Van Halen while care-

fully refining the details
of the cross-country road
trip we'd take as soon as
we were old enough. Our
plan was to hitch a U-Haul
trailer to the back of my car
and fill it full of cans of soup.
To save money, of course.
And we wanted a covered
trailer, not an open one, to
keep our soup safe.

The astounding thing is that
two brains had been working on
this and neither one noticed any
oversights. For instance, would it not have been better to
buy a can of soup in each town instead of renting a trailer
for ten dollars a day plus mileage, filling it with several
hundred pounds of metal and condensed tomato sauce,
increasing gas consumption, and causing horrendous
damage to the bumper and undercarriage of the car that I
didn't even own yet?

In the middle of our fine-tuning the world's worst
idea, my mother phoned to tell me that I had failed eighth
grade. The school counselor had just called her. Had

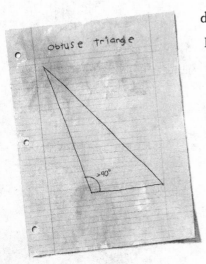

school officials been eavesdropping on Michele and me? Had they decided that anyone making plans to haul canned soup from coast to coast wasn't quite ready for the world, or even ninth grade and its obtuse triangles? After all, "an obtuse triangle is a triangle in which one of the angles is an obtuse angle."*

I was upset. So far, there had been no major consequences to my behavior. Not passing eighth grade was the first roadblock I hit that I couldn't distract people from or charm away. I was going to stay in junior high while all my friends went on to high school to learn about this obtuse triangle.

When I went back in the fall for my second eighth grade, I felt like a caged animal. I saw my classmates as lowly seventh graders, but as a failure, I couldn't feel too superior. And worse yet, my mother was furious.

---

* http://mathworld.wolfram.com/ObtuseTriangle.html

At first she responded by being much more on top of checking in on whether I'd done my homework, but she wasn't able to do it for long. It was as draining for her to stay on top of me about my homework as it was for me to do it.

My second eighth grade turned out to be great socially, and a lot of the people I considered lowly seventh graders are my good friends to this day. Still, l couldn't muster up any sort of interest in what the adult humans at the front of our classes were saying to our teenaged faces. Part of me was so embarrassed by being held back that I couldn't bring myself to try harder. So I became even more of a class clown to distract everyone from my failure. I got big laughs reading aloud our chalkboard's pronoun lesson as "He . . . She . . . It" and then "He she-it," and finally merging it into a very loud "HE SHIT!" I also was of the mind that if my teachers were going to keep me down with their grade books, I was going to do my best to keep them down and get some laughs while I was at it. In one science class, my teacher sat at the back of the class, directly behind me so he could keep an eye on me while our science movie was projected onto a screen at the front of the room. I turned around and stared at his face. He told me to turn around and watch the movie, to which I replied, "I am," to which he replied, "No, you're not, you need to turn around and watch the movie." After several rounds of this, he asked how I could possibly be watching the movie while I was looking at him, and I said, "I'm watching it in the reflection of your glasses." By that point, the kids in the back of the classroom had all their attention on us. Furious, my teacher jumped up from his seat and sent me to the principal's office with a discipline referral that stated, "When asked to turn around and watch the movie, Tig said to me 'I'm watching in the reflection of your glasses.'" I walked right past the door to the principal's office, my regular stomping grounds, and headed to the library, where I hung out, acting like I was reading books. Which is not, apparently, how you pass your second eighth grade.

When I failed my second eighth grade, I was humiliated. Considering all I've been through as a grown adult, it still holds up as one of the darker moments of my life. The loser seventh graders had moved beyond me, and I was now about to be with those mega-loser sixth graders. When you've been through as many eighth grades as I have, you stop remembering the details. I can only tell you that I was three years older than everybody and still in eighth grade. Thankfully, school officials gave me an automatic pass to ninth grade, probably to prevent me from hurling myself off of a building.

I was in ninth grade in In-School Suspension (ISS) when I had my epiphany. Most of my friends had gone off to college, and I was sitting in a cubicle, in a confined classroom where I'd been told to sit all day. Half a dozen isolated cubicles were occupied by the other hardened criminals, guilty of chewing gum, running through the halls, and talking in class. My teachers had my classwork delivered to my cubicle, and if the classwork was not finished by the end of the day, I would be assigned another day of ISS plus that day's classwork. I stared at the growing stacks of work and textbooks I'd never seen before, though they apparently belonged to me, and wondered who on earth they thought was going to be doing this work. I felt totally trapped. And then it hit me: "Oh, I can just leave. I can just quit school." No one can legally force me to be here anymore. I got up from my cubicle and started walking empty-handed toward the hallway. The overweight gym coach who was in charge of babysitting us stepped in front of the door saying, "Whoa, whoa, whoa, where do you think you're going?"

"I'm headin' home," I said.

"No, you're not allowed to leave until you've finished your work," he said.

"No, I'm heading home. Like, I quit. I'm done. I'm leaving," I told him.

He was absolutely bewildered. It felt amazing. The heavens opened. The chains came off. I could go back to leisurely reading *Ribsy* without guilt. I was seventeen and had figured out that I had freedom and power. It wasn't the first time I'd made my way around an out-of-shape gym coach in a doorway, but by God, it would be the last.

I don't remember much about telling my mother and Ric I was dropping out, but their general reaction was a hands-in-the-air "we give up," and "do what you want."

Keeping me in school was an exhausting battle. I think for all of us my dropping out was similar to the death of a loved one with a long-term illness. It offered them a complicated sense of relief. My mother, in particular, welcomed the end of the battle and switched gears completely. She was soon bragging that I had dropped out of school and was off doing my own thing. I'm not sure what she thought that meant. I had nothing going on. I mean, I was shooting pool, playing guitar, and selling po' boys. I didn't know anyone else who was doing those exact three things, so maybe that's what left her beaming with pride. The only thing that would make me more perfect in my mother's eyes was if I got my GED. I guess she was just feeling like she needed to make sure I had all the suppos-

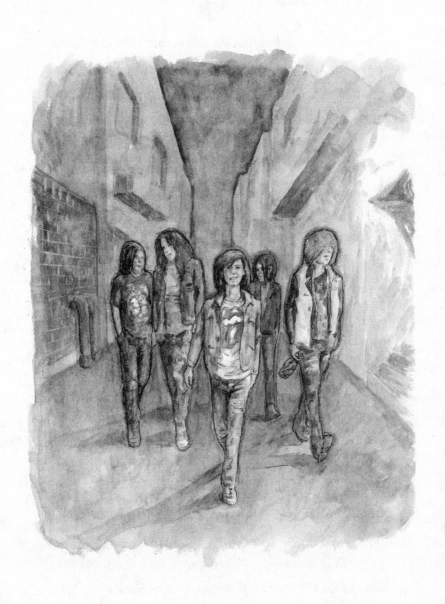

edly necessary things that she pretty much hated, too. So a year later, at age eighteen, I bubbled in enough of the right answers on a Scantron to pass and get a GED, and then I tossed the certificate of my very general knowledge into a box, along with records and tennis shoes, and threw it all in the trunk of my car. I felt there was nothing left for me in Houston and was anxious to make a whole new life someplace else.

I had chosen Denver, Colorado, mainly because my mother had briefly attended college in Gunnison and had painted Colorado as an utter paradise. Heading west with Texas in my rearview mirror, I was overcome with fits of utter glee and maniacal laughter as it hit me, over and over, that I would never have to wake up and go to school ever again. It was empowering to think that I would finally be responsible for everything good and bad that was going to happen to me. I didn't have big dreams. The thought of my own very simple life, where I made just enough to support myself, was thrilling.

I had been eager to live on my own since I was fifteen, when I had started looking at apartments and figuring out my budget from my $3.15 an hour job at a day-care center. As I said, it wasn't a glamorous life I'd been dreaming about.

TIG'S MONTHLY BUDGET, 1986
Rent: $150
Gasoline: $15
Electricity: $15
Phone/Long-Distance Calls: $30
Cigarettes: $100*
Food: $80
Snacks: $5
Rock Concerts: $12.50

And it wasn't a glamorous life that I found in Denver, either, but it was *my* life—all of it—and I got to do what I wanted with it, which was to make it my version of perfect. I loved getting down on my hands and knees and scrubbing the grit from my studio's kitchen floor. I lived in a generic apartment in a generic building. Nobody would see where I lived and say, *"Oooohhh!"*—unless, for some reason, I invited them inside and they saw all twenty square feet of my gleaming linoleum floor.

I found more work in child care and lived proudly

---

*Assuming I worked a forty-hour workweek at $3.15 per hour, I was over budget by at least $7.50 (before taxes) and would have to plan on bumming cigarettes for the last several days of every month.

within or below my pathetic means, check-to-check, hand-to-mouth, mouth-to-something-I-got-on-discount. I regularly looked through all the newspaper ads and clipped deals on things like pudding, bread, cheese—all the staples. I never went out to eat because there would be no pride in eating a sandwich I didn't make. And let's be honest, I couldn't afford it.

I searched for the perfect new friends to share my two-for-one pickles with. I loved music and wanted to be in a band, so I put an ad in the paper looking for anyone who played guitar, and then I headed to coffee shops, poetry readings, music venues, and all sorts of open mics, in search of my new pals. I did eventually find my core friends, who I've remained close with over the years, but my search often had me returning to my apartment discouraged and emotionally exhausted, wishing deeply that I could call up an old friend and say, "Hey, wanna come over and look at my immaculate floors, and I'll tell you about all my adventures in trying to find a new you?"

By twenty-four, I had moved to Austin and then back to Denver, this time to a much cooler part of the city and with my cat, Bunny. Each day I treated Bunny to brown pellets I poured from a bag that boasted CAT FOOD in bold black print. I would have found the complete simple, good, and affordable life I was hoping for if only an aisle over I could've grabbed a bag of HUMAN FOOD as well. One day, I came home to discover that Bunny had a taste for something even less refined than CAT FOOD. She was resting on my kitchen table, surrounded by little bits of chewed-up paper, which I realized were the corners of the certificate that was supposed to be helping me get further along in life. I sat back and started processing what had happened: My cat ate my GED. To my delight, I saw that she had then used the litter box. It tickled me on the deepest level to imagine being required to present this document at a possible future job interview:

Proof of education?

Sure, here's the main part, and here's the chewed-up corners, and here's what I scooped out of the litter box.

In the meantime, I had found work in the music industry without needing a single scrap of my GED. I

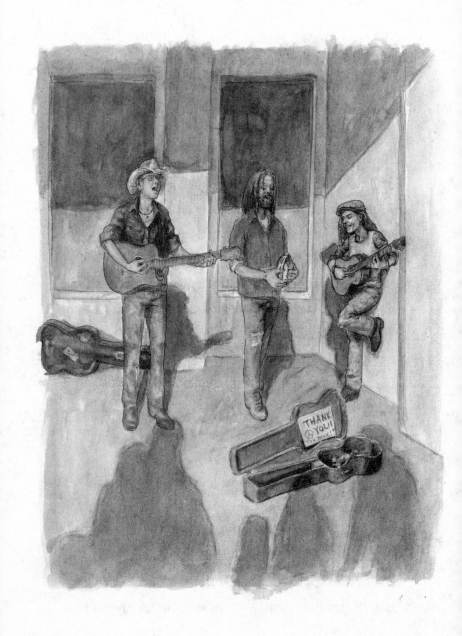

promoted and booked bands both independently and for an indie rock label out of Chicago, in hopes of possibly starting my own music management business one day. I was still making very little money, but I felt on my way to finding my place in the world. Sometimes it seemed I wasn't headed in exactly the right direction, but when I looked around at my life and where I was, I had a feeling of *If this is as good as it gets, it's not that bad.*

I framed what was left of my GED with a new sense of pride for what it stood for: Just because people say you need a certain thing for a successful life, doesn't also mean that very thing can't eventually be crapped out by your cat and then scooped up and tossed into a trash can and hauled away to a toxic landfill.

Okay, so maybe it *was* a glamorous life I was living after all. But with all the glamour came isolation. It's lonely at the top.

3

The Downfall

I never had any intention of moving to Los Angeles. Not only had working in the world of television and film never really spoken to me, I thought Los Angeles was strictly A-list celebrities hanging out on Hollywood Boulevard and then, beyond that, *Cops. Cops,* as in the reality-TV show where they kick down doors, everyone screams, everyone tries to run, everyone gets arrested, and then of course, there's the rabid dog in the yard, chained to a tree stump eating a metal garbage can. Who would have guessed such a place would hold the key to my happiness and the people who I would relate to most, none of whom you'd ever find on Hollywood Boulevard or in an episode of *Cops?* (Side note: I don't mean to blow the surprise, but before you set aside your life savings to visit Hollywood Boulevard, I feel obligated to tell you that it's crawling with an unsavory clientele going in and out of the likes of Kentucky Fried Chicken, and the famous sidewalk stars are covered in sunbaked urine and empty gum wrappers. Put it this way: Picture the grossest area of the town you live in, and it's likely worse than that. But if this sounds appealing to you, then by all means.)

Yet, after two years of living in Denver, I somehow found myself in a U-Haul with my childhood friends Beth and Leslie, moving ourselves and our crinkly lampshades and muddy hiking boots to Los Angeles. I had more of a reason to follow them than not. They were my closest friends and were pursuing their dreams of working in film and television, and I was pursuing my dream of someday having a dream.

Two weeks after we moved to Los Angeles, I was on-stage at Little Frida's Coffee House in West Hollywood doing stand-up for the first time.

It was the most exhilarating, addicting, and surreal experience. The fact that an audience of thirty people was laughing was even more surreal—and distracting. Obviously, if you're doing stand-up, you want laughs, but I had not accounted for laughs. I just knew I had a story to get out there—the time I called a stranger to get tickets for a show, and he misunderstood my name as "Pig" and kept calling me that until I awkwardly corrected him in person. Besides music, stand-up was something I had always followed and fantasized about doing, but I had never considered it a dream within my reach. It seemed like a dream only a chosen few, snatched from some exclusive part of the universe, could pursue; as unlikely a profession for me as becoming president.

After my first "set," I left the coffee shop doing leprechaun kicks. I had found my dream so quickly: doing open mics for the rest of my life! Bigger dreams, such as being a rhythm-guitar player in a touring band could wait. For now, my eyes were peeled for faded sign-up sheets taped to the walls of bars and coffee shops around town. Several months into my career as an open-miker I realized that, for the most part, the stand-up scene was a far more concentrated group of the smart, interesting, eccentric, and funny people that I'd always liked to surround myself with—a congregation of oddballs indeed from some special part of the universe. I began to refer to the comedy scene as "the land of misfit toys." It was comforting to be surrounded by people who didn't fit into the confines of society, and it was the first time in my life that I wasn't met with the boring conversation stopper: "Oh my God, you're so weird."

Sarah Silverman was the first comic friend I made who was well beyond my level of experience. I had been in Los Angeles about a year when she walked up and complimented my corduroy pants at a mutual friend's party. I complimented her outfit, not as a return gesture but because I really liked her style. A moment later, we discovered that we both liked the same comedians and the color green. When it was revealed that we were both die-hard Chrissie Hynde fans, we took ourselves to a corner for a passionate game of Who's Your Favorite, What's Your Favorite. It was a little later than I planned, but I'd finally met the person who should've been my sixth-grade best friend. As we left the party, trying to go our separate ways, we discovered we lived off of the same street and in walking distance from each other's house. There was an unspoken: *That's it. You and me from this day on, but not really until we run into each other again three years from now in New York City. See ya then, kid!*

In December of 2011, my career and personal life were as good as I could have imagined them to be. I was in a new relationship, I had a full tour schedule, and my close friend of over a decade, Sarah Silverman, had written a role for me to play myself in her new NBC pilot, *Susan 313*, executive-produced by Ron Howard.

Even though Sarah had written the part for me, I still needed to be officially hired by the network and the studio, which meant auditioning like everyone else. You'd think auditioning to play yourself would be an easy gig to snag, but the pressure was intense. How do you not get a part written for you by the star of the show? (I hear this actually happens all the time, so that's what I'm going to believe.) Also, auditioning scares me because I feel like an impostor. I'm not an "actor," I'm a comedian, and almost all the work I'd ever gotten was from a friend hiring me. I began to worry that having the part written for me would work against me and the network would find several other people who could play the role of "Tig" better than I could. Sarah set things up so I didn't have to audition in person for the network, I just had to go put myself on tape doing a scene with Sarah in a twenty-foot-by-twenty-foot room in front of several writers, the director, a casting director, two personal assistants, and the president of Imagine Entertainment. Eh, no big deal.

Sarah had done everything in her power to make this audition as seamless as possible. Before I auditioned to play myself, she reassured me that everyone in the room was rooting for me and that we'd run my lines as many times as it took to get the perfect take. I messed up a few lines here and there. No sweat. We started over. And over. And over. And over. And over. And over. I began to feel my face flush. What was my problem?! This part was written for me! This was *me*! I had learned the lines like the back of my hand. Sarah was beautifully lobbing her lines over to me, and I was fumbling almost every single one of them. I began to feel a full-blown anxiety attack coming on. Not only did I want this role, but I was desperate to be as good as Sarah thought I was. And then came my freak-out. Mid-poorly-delivered-line, I pulled the mic off my shirt and said, "I can't do this." I walked off camera and sat down with my head between my hands. I was on the verge of tears. I mean, had I forgotten what it was like to have real problems? Boo-hoo, my life is rife with opportunity.

I was trying to perfect "me," but try after try, I was becoming someone I didn't even recognize. My instinct was to run out the door and drive my car home, directly back to Mississippi, and start over completely in life. But here I was with a roomful of industry big shots staring at me while I sat before them with my head in my hands, muttering, "I can't do this, I can't do this . . ." (Reminder: I had been Tig for forty years—nonstop.) Surely they were thinking what I was thinking: *God, somebody sucks at being Tig.*

Still, these were all decent human beings who cheered me on and kept their thoughts to themselves. After a long, awkward five minutes in the tiny room, Sarah said, "Look, this time, let's just try to get your worst possible takes." And so I did my worst takes over and over until I got it right. And I got the part of me. Barely.

When you're struggling to secure the role of yourself, you do wonder whether you know who you are. Up until that audition, I had felt confident I did.

I had been a road comic, touring incessantly around the world for more than ten years, and felt I could perform before pretty much any kind of audience, having realized I'd always had my voice and perspective and had just needed to cultivate the confidence to express them. In fact, improvising with the audience, maintaining my cool, and turning any foibles into highlights were all things I had thought were my strengths.

Walking away from the audition, I had the impression that NBC might know specific nuances about me that I was unaware of. Ultimately, it was a moot point. Not only did the show not get picked up to series, but my life, myself, was all about to change.

After Sarah's pilot was cast and shot, I starred in a play, filmed a movie, and toured the country on my "days off." February 28 was the end of a two-month-long tour and the last day I was totally fine. I was looking forward to March 1, when my episode of *The Office* would air—a date that I will remember forever because the first crack in what I thought was a seamless life and career showed up as a tickle in my throat.

On March 2, my throat was still sore, and I was congested, coughing, and dehydrated. I had a headache, a fever, and no appetite, and I got steadily worse as each day passed. After a week, it felt like no amount of fluids or rest was helping. Brooke, my girlfriend of five months, took me to urgent care, where I was given antibiotics and a shot of penicillin and diagnosed with bronchitis and a severe sinus infection. That's when my health really began to go downhill. Brooke didn't feel comfortable leaving me by myself at home and would call friends of mine to come sit with me while she went to work or ran to the store. She was terrified something horrible would happen to me. I acted like she was overreacting, but truth be told, I never get sick, and I was terrified something horrible would happen to me, too. How often, in a couple of weeks, does a relatively young and seemingly healthy person have to hear, "Don't get up. We're going to get you a wheelchair" before she knows something is seriously wrong?

Brooke took me to urgent care again, where I was hooked up to an IV for severe dehydration, but returning home pumped with fluids didn't help at all. My tongue was like sandpaper. Smiling, which wasn't happening often, meant getting my lips stuck to my gums.

Before and after my second trip to urgent care, I fulfilled my obligation (against everyone's wishes) to shoot a role in my friend Lake Bell's movie *In a World*. Between takes, I slept in an isolated upstairs rest area they had set up for me. Anytime I came down to shoot my scene, I had to harness the inner strength of a thousand humans. No one could have guessed how ill I felt. I guess I was a good actor after all. On my last day on set, my gut began to distend and shoot with pain. It was a dull, almost unbearable ache, which continued for the next few days and made fastening my pants torturous and keeping food in my system nearly impossible. Anything I ate was finding a way out of me, anywhere it could and as soon as possible.

On March 12, four days after I left the set of *In a*

World, the ache in my gut brought me to my knees, and I collapsed while walking down Brooke's stairs. She drove me straight to the emergency room, and I was immediately put on Dilaudid—a painkiller also known as "hospital heroin," which is about five times stronger than morphine. My closest friends showed up, and doctors came and went. Then a doctor came in who told me he had the results from some scans he had taken and asked if I would like to be alone or with my friends when he explained them. I saw my friends Beth and Kyle exchange glances like they couldn't believe things were so serious that they needed to leave the room. This was the one time I hoped to be told in public that I simply had gas. In case the doctor was going to tell me I was dying, I told my friends that I'd like to be alone for the news.

After the room was clear of friends, the doctor informed me that the scans revealed fluid in my lungs, which meant that the sinus infection and bronchitis had turned into pneumonia. "Oh," I thought, "I must've finally gotten the thing I was supposed to get in seventh grade when I went outside with my hair wet." I did think pneumonia was serious, but I only had a moment to think about it before the doctor went on to explain how they originally thought my abdominal pain meant that I also had appendicitis, but there was so much swelling in my gut that my organs could not be identified. Instead of sending me to the pharmacy with a prescription for a long swig of a pink chalky drink like I thought he would, the doctor admitted me to the hospital immediately.

Forty-eight hours later, after lots of tests, the doctors still did not know what was wrong with me. Finally, a doctor told my girlfriend and me that he would test me for *Clostridium difficile* (C-diff), adding that he didn't think it was likely that I had it, since it's the very sickly and elderly who usually get it, and that we should certainly hope I did not have it. The following day the results came in. I had tested positive for C-diff, and it had spread throughout my entire digestive tract. C-diff is an overgrowth of the *Clostridium difficile* bacteria, which attack the intestinal lining, and it can kill you. Many contract C-diff by accidentally ingesting the spores in a hospital or other medical facility and/or by taking antibiotics and having their "good" bacteria cleared out, allowing the C-diff to flourish. The doctor informed me that the antibiotics I'd been given a week earlier were likely the cause of my C-diff, which was severe. The Dilaudid unplugged me and left me feeling as though I was operating on 5 percent of my battery, so when I heard this news, it was all I could do to keep a single eye open. Brooke, upon hearing it, breathed a sigh of relief, feeling we were lucky to finally have a name for what was wrong with me. Neither of us really understood what horrific news we had just received.

After three comalike days in the hospital, the surgeon told me it was likely they were going to have to remove a good portion of my intestines due to the severity of my case. Highly drugged, I slurred, "Okay," as if it was totally fine to have most of my intestines removed. I was lying in bed with little information, unable to understand most of what I was overhearing or being told. I slept, mumbled conversations with friends, and watched them interact without me. Mostly I read the dry-erase board in front me:

Dilaudid 2 P.M.
Dilaudid 4 P.M.
Dilaudid 6 P.M.
Dilaudid 8 P.M.
Dilaudid 10 P.M.
Dilaudid 12 A.M.
Discharge Date: ??

I was so unaware of what was happening that I thought the six to eight of my closest friends who had been camped out at my bedside, day and night, were there to keep me from being bored, since my only real activity was getting my sandpaper tongue sponged with water. I had no idea they were at times crying outside my room wondering what part of their bodies they could donate if I needed an organ and asking each other, "Do you think she's going to live?" and "Should we call her mom?" (Which they'd have to do swiftly because, at that point, she had only two weeks to live.)

After eight days in the hospital, my body finally responded to the medication, and I tested negative for C-diff, meaning it was now in remission. I could leave as soon as I was able to keep solid food in my system, but when a meal tray was placed in front of me, I looked down, thinking, "What beast would possibly be able to ingest all of this?" Casually eating a whole meal seemed superhuman. My body would no longer accept two tiny bites of toast and a green bean, which meant that I had twenty-four more hours of reading the word "Dilaudid" and feeling the agonizing pain of it wearing off before a nurse came to refill it. The following day, with half a cup of applesauce securely in my stomach, I left the hospital in yet another wheelchair, feeling anxious and excited to get back to my life and leave that horrible blip in time behind.

This happened right before my forty-first birthday. A few days after I got out of the hospital, I had to have my assistant Aaron drive me around to do errands for the small birthday party I was throwing. I might have tested negative for C-diff and been released from the hospital, but I was not okay. I still could not keep food in my system and was in the kind of pain that had me constantly gripping my stomach and confined mostly to bed. My mother called to wish me a happy birthday, but I missed her call. As usual, her voice mail was lively and playful:

> *"Tig, Ric and I want to come out to California.*
> Happy birthday to you. Happy birthday to you.
> Happy birthday, dear Fluff. Happy birthday to
> you. *I love you. Ric loves you, too, and we want to*
> *come out and visit. I'll let Ric talk to you . . ."*

The last time I talked to my mother, I had been lying in bed too sick to eat or sit up. She knew I wasn't feeling well and was calling to tell me to drink orange juice and to generally check on me, aka "Fluff" (the nickname my messy hair inspired every morning of my childhood). I hadn't told her, or anyone in my family, how sick I was because I didn't want anyone to worry, and also, I had no real idea how sick I was.

Two days after I missed my mother's call, I decided to drive Brooke to work. I wasn't feeling better in the slightest, but since time was passing, I felt like I should go through the motions of being better. I dropped her off and was pulling out of the Sunset Gower Studio lot when my phone rang and "parents" popped up on my caller ID. I assumed it was my mother calling to see how I was feeling and wish me a belated happy birthday. I scrambled to grab the call, but I missed it and it went to voice mail. I had a service that translated my voice mails to text messages, and as I pulled out onto Sunset Boulevard, I glanced down at my cell:

> *"Hi Tig, this is Ric. I'm afraid I have some
> terrible news for you. Your mother fell last night,
> and it looks like she's not going to make it. Please
> give me a call. Thank you."*

I thought I was reading it wrong, or that I was not comprehending something simple. What did he mean, "she's not going to make it"? She was still alive now, right? Wasn't she getting help? I reread the text over and over, trying to make sense of it, because it seemed that Ric was saying my mother was going to die and Ric never exaggerates or minces words. *This must be the truth: My mother is dying.* I pictured her lying in a hospital bed, conscious and struggling, saying she wants to see me to say good-bye.

I drove around the block, frantically repeating, "Oh my God, oh my God, oh my God," as I called Brooke to tell her the news. I headed back to the studio lot, parked, and, shaking and sick to my stomach, called Ric back. Calmly, but in a voice heavy with emotion, he explained that the night before, my mother had tripped on the end table, fallen, and hit her head on the tile floor. He said she got up and was conscious and talking. After checking her head and staying up with her for a little while, he decided she was fine and went to bed while she stayed in the living room watching Jimmy Kimmel.

The next morning—this very morning—Ric said he got up and saw the TV still on and the back of my mother still sitting in her chair. He told me that he walked around to the front of her chair and saw that blood was coming out of her nose and mouth. He said she was breathing, but not conscious, and that he shook her and yelled her name over and over. What could I have possibly been doing when all of this was happening? Mustering the strength to get out of bed? Looking for my pants with the drawstring? I'd spent my entire morning pretending I wasn't still feeling weak, forcing myself to believe I was ready to pick up my life where I'd left off.

I looked out my window at all the other cars parked in the studio lot and asked, "Can I talk to her?" He said, "No, Tig. You can't. You won't ever be able to talk to her again."

"What are you talking about?" I demanded. "There's no chance?" It was absolutely impossible that I could never talk to my mother again. It's my *mother*. Ric gave me the facts, but he was not speaking in his usual matter-of-fact tone. It sounded like all the life had been kicked out of him as he told me that she had suffered massive hemorrhaging and that there had been so much blood that her brain had been pushed entirely to one side, that she had zero chance of recovery. I asked if my brother, Renaud, knew, and he said he'd tried to call him, but his voice mail was full. Ric doesn't know how to text, so I hung up and texted my brother to call me immediately. My brother called moments later, and I sobbed as I told him exactly what Ric had just told me. Renaud processed the news stoically while seeming to be in as much shock as I was, accepting every incomprehensible piece of information with "Oh my God, okay . . ." We needed to make travel plans to fly to Texas, so I explained very briefly that I had been in the hospital with a very serious bacterial infection and was not able to travel until I went back to the hospital and was checked out by a doctor.

"You can't do this, Tig!" Renaud yelled. "You have to tell us this stuff!" I knew his anger was mostly misdirected, but I yelled back because I didn't want to talk about my health. Who cared about my stupid health? I had assumed I was fine and slowly but surely on the mend, and now all that was beside the point. Way beside the point. I continued to cry hysterically, perhaps for both of us. As calmly as he could, Renaud told me he was hanging up and needed to call Ric and that he would call me back.

Feeling nauseated, I crawled into the backseat of the car and lay on my side, tucked into a fetal position, and continued to cry hysterically. How could it be that in less than ten days I was experiencing the worst physical and emotional pain of my life? Brooke walked up to the car, and talked to me through the half-open window. "I'm so sorry, babe," she said while I sobbed and told her everything I'd just heard. "I'm so sorry, babe," she said again. I assumed she was in shock, which surely she was, but I would soon discover that while nurturing people physically came naturally to her, our relationship was too new, and our connection not yet deep enough, for the degree of emotional depth and support I would need. And even if our bond had been stronger, I now know that there is simply not any person at any point in time who can truly console you when you have received the news that your mother is dying.

Lying down and crying in the backseat of the car, I felt like a child, and I wanted to be cared for like a child. Nothing Brooke said or offered up seemed to be a place I could rest, especially when she invited me to come hang out in her office while my mother lay dying in Texas. Sitting at a big conference table among all her busy coworkers was the last place I wanted to be. I told her I had to call some people and called an ex-girlfriend in Ohio who had known my mother. Brooke stood outside the car window for the half hour I talked on the phone. I could see in her face that she wished she knew what to do. As consumed as I was by my devastation, I still felt a sliver of rage that Brooke's first instinct wasn't to ask for the day off from work to be with me, even if she was scared to since she'd already taken off work when I was in the hospital.

When she realized I wasn't going to hang out in her office among her coworkers, Brooke did finally ask for the day off. I booked a flight for later that evening and then we went to the doctor's so I could get some more testing and the proper medications for travel. I'd been losing a half pound a day since I'd last left the hospital and was still severely dehydrated and having regular stabbing pains in my gut. Brooke lay on my bed as I put my clothes in a suitcase, and I realized I wasn't just packing to go visit my mother in a hospital. I was also packing for her funeral. I don't live my life feeling like a victim, but I suddenly felt very sorry for myself. I had lost so much weight that my pants were falling off; I had diarrhea every ten minutes; and now I was choosing what to wear to my mother's funeral while she was still alive. It all seemed completely wrong and cruel. Packing my bag, I became filled with guilt, thinking I was giving up on my mother and losing hope, even though I'd been told there was absolutely no hope.

My mother had been in a coma once before and almost died. She was on a date in Gunnison, Colorado, and her date lost control of the car going over Monarch Pass. She flew through the windshield and ended up in a ditch and then in a coma, having broken almost every bone in her body. Her prognosis wasn't promising, but family and friends maintained hope. Although the accident would leave her with lifelong, full-body, chronic pain, she recovered rather quickly. To celebrate, her aunt Googsie and uncle Rory took her and her then–best friend, Tina, on a road trip to the Grand Canyon. Still on crutches with a broken leg, my mother wrapped her able leg through the railing at the edge, and hung backward into the canyon with her arms stretched out. Years later, after she married Ric, she still had all the screws the doctors had used to straighten her toes and found it hilarious to have friends over for cocktails and serve them martinis with a twist— you know, as in with an olive on a long, thin screw. Her friends would say, "Susie, this is so cool! What made you think to do this?"

"Oh, those are the screws they used to straighten my broken toes after the accident," she'd say, absolutely loving to watch her guests' polite shock at learning where exactly the whimsical metal accoutrement they were admiring had been before it stabbed the gourmet olive they were nibbling on.

"And the bowl you're eating nuts out of," she'd say, almost bursting with pride, "was the vomit tray that I threw up into." There are so many parts of me that are like my mother, and then yet parts of me have no resemblance to her whatsoever. I love to shock people. I would use screws that had been in my toes for my friends' cocktails. But I would never hang upside down above the

Grand Canyon. Nor would I stay up all night and toast the sunrise with friends from around the neighborhood as my children's alarm clocks went off for school.

A few hours later, I was aboard a plane on my way to say good-bye to my mother and take her off life support. It had only been nine hours since I thought my biggest problem was that my tummy still hurt. Waiting to take off, I had a strong need for more emotional comfort before being squeezed among strangers and alone with my thoughts for two and a half hours. So I ran off the plane and into the Jetway to call Sascha, a very compassionate person who I had dated prior to Brooke. When I told her my mother was dying, she told me that one of the things that had always attracted her to me was my strength, and that while she knew this was incredibly difficult, she also knew I would get through it. As simple as what she said was, it helped me, and I had begun to feel like I could make it through my flight when a flight attendant poked her head out and told me to get back on the plane. I turned to her and said, "I'm sorry, my mother is dying—" This was the first time I had said this to a stranger, and it felt surreal. The news of my mother's fall, telling my friends about it, buying a plane ticket, packing and going to the airport had all happened in some kind of dreamlike state of denial where the hope of her recovery still floated around my mind. But speaking the truth to someone outside of my circle woke me from denial into the bizarre nightmare that was reality: My mother is dying.

"Please, do what you have to do," the flight attendant said, and put her hands up. "Take as long as you need." Then she ducked back into the plane. Her brief kindness touched me deeply. It was a real human moment that the FAA couldn't regulate.

I arrived in Houston at midnight and met my brother at the airport. We got into a taxi together and began to make small talk. Who was he dating? Who was I dating? How was his job? Had I been touring a lot? How long had I been in the hospital? What were some of the details of my illness, and was I going to be okay? My brother and I have had varying degrees of closeness over the years, but was this really the time to start to get to know each other? I guess so. It was absurd to think that even with the impending death of our mother, our guards were still up. We might as well have included the cabdriver in our conversation. Who was *he* dating?

We mentioned our mother, of course, but it was a stoic and stunned conversation with both of us looking straight ahead. Neither of us knew how to face her death and funeral. The plan for now was to just get to the house, go to sleep, and visit her in the morning.

The only reason my mother was on life support was so that we could see her while she was still alive. I don't know why I needed to see someone who wasn't really there anymore, but I would have felt more cheated by her death if I hadn't been able to see her, even in that state. I needed to see with my own eyes that she was in some sort of irreversible sleep state, and would never respond to me, or anyone, again. My whole life, anytime I tapped my mother to awaken her, her eyes would open. Somewhere in me, I hoped there would be a miracle moment where all I had to do was tap her and she would, if not come completely back, at least be able to say good-bye.

I guess, like most people, I couldn't accept death—or impending death—without a body. As a kid, I had fantasies about finding Amelia Earhart alive. I'd hire a pilot and, luckily, it'd be a pretty direct flight since I'd always imagined us spotting her on her tiny sand island just hours after takeoff. We'd land and she'd start jumping up and down and waving wildly, wearing her ragged I've-been-stranded-on-an-island jeans.

When I walked into Ric and my mother's house that night, I stared down at the floor. I didn't want to see any pictures of my mother or the chair where she lost consciousness, or even the hallway that led to her bedroom. I walked straight back to my room, and right into a group of framed photos of my mother on my dresser. Now I had to look at them. I picked each one up and stared at it and began to sob all over again. When I got into bed, I just lay there, hearing the sound of her head hitting the floor over and over. I kept wanting to somehow stop her fall or run over to her afterward, while she sat in her chair seeming fine, and tell her she needed to go to the hospital, that she needed to go right now.

My stomach flashed with pain, and I was drained from the effort of just walking around with no nutrients in my system. The only thing I was really capable of doing was lying down. But I could only sleep for moments at a time. The following day I would have to go to the hospital, take her off life support, and let her die. It was what she would want and now it was in my hands.

As a child, I was the world's tiniest party bummer, riding my bike over to my mother's friends' houses whenever my self-parenting skills came up short and I needed some assistance—you know, help with reaching, spelling, cutting the crust off of bread, or getting a ride somewhere that my bike couldn't take me.

While I lay in bed dozing off for a second here or there, I was battered by the thought that tomorrow my mother's party would officially be over, and how tremendously unprepared I felt for the terrible responsibility of sending her home this time.

4

Saying Good-Bye

On the mornings when my mother hadn't been up all night, she would yell for me to wake up, and I would stay in bed, shouting that I was up, and then fall back asleep and miss the school bus. Eventually, I'd hear, "I don't hear anything!" and I'd retort with "I'm up!" What was I expecting? I couldn't see fifteen minutes into the future when she'd bust my door open and ask what the hell I was doing. I'd fly out of bed, put on whatever clothes were nearby, and head out the door looking like I'd just woken up, because I had. My mother would drive me to school at least thirty miles per hour over the speed limit, and I would sit in the front seat, silently staring out the window while she yelled for me to pull it together and to start giving a damn. I did not give a damn. But I did wonder when *she* would pull it together and start giving a damn.

This morning's ride was silent. Ric drove, and my brother sat in the front seat while I sat in the back, watching downtown Houston rush past us. I had just rolled out of bed, but I definitely gave a damn. Every moment of the car ride, I tried to prepare myself for what my mother would look like and how it would feel to see her.

No one spoke walking down the halls toward her room. And no amount of Ric's warnings about how upsetting it would be to see her, unresponsive and hooked up to a machine, with tubes running in and out of her, helped. When he pulled back the curtain around her bed, I felt hollow, as though I'd lost every ounce of everything in me. Ric stayed at the foot of her bed and Renaud and I stood on either side of it. We all began sobbing. No one embraced anyone. That my mother had been the lively, affectionate member of our family was now clearer than it had ever been. Tentatively, I put my hand on her arm and then on her hand, afraid to discover what I already knew: Nothing was going to happen when I touched her. It was one of the most confusing moments of my life to see her breathing, even if not on her own, and to be crying and talking to her and touching her, and have her not wake up.

An hour later, a doctor informed us that whenever

we were ready to take her off the respirator to let him
know. We gave each other a moment alone with her and
then let the nurses into her room. All of us left and stood
in the hall. We heard nothing. Ten minutes later, the
nurses came out of her room and said the life support had
been removed and we could go back in if we wanted to.
I thought that people died as soon as they were taken off
life support, but that is not always the case. My mother
looked the same, but without the tubes, she looked like
she was sleeping. Her breaths came every eight to ten
seconds.

I called Maxine, one my mother's closest friends, if
not *the* closest, and asked her to come to the hospital,
knowing that her presence would be like having a piece
of my mother in the room. "Oh, Susie, oh, Susie," Maxine said in disbelief when she arrived and saw my mother
lying there. She went on about how beautiful my mother
looked, and how she had always had the best, tightest
skin, and that she still did, right at that moment. A year
later, Maxine would reveal that she had wanted to take a
photo of my mother that day, because she felt like even
that moment was a part of my mother's story, and she
wanted me to have a picture of it because every moment
of my mother's life was important. And I would have

loved to have that photo, but I know my mother wouldn't have wanted a picture of herself taken when she was in that condition—no matter how good her skin looked.

Maxine stayed with us for about an hour. There was a lot of crying and talking about my mother's youthful beauty, all of us expressing constant disbelief about what had happened. "I can't believe that just two years ago, I called Susie to tell her Sheila died, and now here we are losing your mom," she said. "Who would've guessed we'd lose both of them so quickly?"

Sheila was Maxine's older sister, who had gone in for knee surgery, gotten a blood clot in her lung, and then died from a pulmonary embolism. I had learned all this in a text from my close friend Shannon, who was Sheila's niece and Maxine's daughter. This wasn't just some friend's aunt dying. Anyone who really knew me knew how much Sheila meant to me and how much I loved to hear funny Sheila stories. Early in my comedy career, I told stories about Sheila and repeated lines she'd said, and the audience devoured them. The news of Sheila's death had been the worst thing that had happened in my life since Hurricane Katrina had destroyed my hometown of Pass Christian, Mississippi.

Sheila and Maxine had grown up in Delcambre (pronounced *dell-come*), Louisiana. You know, born on the bayou. Roughly twenty years ago, Sheila moved from Delcambre to Spring, Texas, to live with Maxine and her family. Sheila's eldest daughter, Patrice, had just been murdered and Sheila's marriage fell apart shortly afterward. I met Sheila in the middle of all this turmoil, when I was around sixteen years old. I was immediately drawn to her because she had the energy of a kid, with the driest, funniest sense of humor. Nobody made me laugh harder than Sheila. She would barge into any conversation with a crazier story and a filthier mouth, and could handle more cans of beer than anyone else. She wasn't one of those desperate adults trying to appear cool so kids will think she's cool. She just was.

Sheila and my mother truly cracked each other up. One of my favorite memories is of being in my mother's backyard with Sheila as my mother and Ric were leaving for vacation. Confused, Sheila pointed at a large dog bowl with water in it and said in her thick Cajun accent, "Susie, you gotta dog?" We didn't have a dog. We hadn't had a dog in at least ten years, but my mother explained how she couldn't bring herself to get rid of the bowl, so she made use of it by keeping it filled with water to deter potential thieves on a break-in mission who would hopefully stop dead in their tracks upon seeing an old dog bowl full of dirty water and a floating leaf—evidence of a very scary guard dog. (Beware of Mother Who Still Misses the Family Dog!) Sheila looked at my mother, slowly piecing together what she was going to slam her with. "Well, tell me this," she said. "When you and Ric are outta town, you want me to swing by every day and change the water in the dog bowl for ya?"

Over the years, Sheila had become a close friend and a kind of mother figure to me. She was runner-up for Life of the Party, right behind my mother, but because I had some distance from her, it was easier to appreciate her wild ways. I enjoyed and experienced Sheila the way I imagine other people enjoyed and experienced my mother. When she died, it was the first time I felt like I'd lost a mother.

Before Maxine left, she told stories about the cruise to Mexico she and my mother had recently gone on with all their Cajun pals from Delcambre. She claimed that my mother would get up every morning before everyone else and dive off the diving board, slide down the slide, and swim around the pool. By the time everyone met for breakfast, she would already have a million stories to tell. We all stared at my mother in her lifeless state while Maxine talked. I easily pictured my mother getting up early to go play in the pool before anybody else, like she was three years old, not someone with three years left. Maxine's presence had lifted me, and when she left, my strength seemed to leave with her.

My mother was soon moved downstairs to hospice. We waited for five hours around her bed, and then Ric, who had grown much frailer in the past several years and was undoubtedly feeling the physical and emotional strain of the past few days, announced that he was headed home. My brother decided that Ric shouldn't drive himself and left with him. I was baffled and terrified; I wasn't expecting to be suddenly alone with my mother, whose last breath could happen any moment. I had no idea how to do this on my own, but I just continued sitting on the edge of the chair next to her bed, staring at her chest going up and down. I felt tense and crouched for a type of action I was totally ill-equipped to perform, like I was suddenly a football player ready for the ball to be hiked to the quarterback. I had been under the impression that severe emotional pain numbed the body to physical pain, but as I sat there counting the seconds between my mother's breaths, the pain emanating from my gut was definitely a ten on the pain scale. Occasionally, I forced myself to recline my chair and lie back in order to alleviate my stabbing stomach pangs.

I was still expecting my mother to die pretty peacefully, like people taken off life support in the movies. But what I was about to sit through was nothing like the death scenes I'd seen in *Fried Green Tomatoes* or *Terms of Endearment*. I was in a horror film in which I was trapped alone in a room with my dying mother, who was now gasping for a single breath of air every ten to fifteen seconds while I sat there just staring at her, wondering if that next breath of air would ever even come, caught between desperately wishing it would and desperately wishing it wouldn't. When you're waiting for your mother to breathe again, ten to fifteen seconds is an eternity.

I found myself doing and saying things that I never did or said when my mother was conscious, like running my hand over her hair and forearms and kissing her forehead. I didn't feel like my mother heard or felt me, but I wished desperately for her to know that I was there with her, that I was doing everything she had ever wanted me to do and saying everything she had ever wanted to hear me say. I knew that if she could come back, she would understand and accept that this extreme situation finally made it okay for me to show her how I felt.

I spent a long time sitting beside her apologizing for not accepting her the way she'd always accepted me. I accepted her unspoken apology, which I was sure she would have made, for any unrest she had caused me.

I remembered a bad fight we had a decade earlier. Our argument was going nowhere and she wanted to get off of the phone. Finally, feeling like she had no other option, she abruptly handed the phone to Ric while I was midsentence. "Tig, your mother doesn't want to talk to you," Ric said, and hung up on me. Nobody answered the phone when I called back. I felt incredibly rejected and abandoned. Now, as I stared at her lifeless body, really understanding that she would have no more chances in this life to do good or bad, I knew that we would both do or give anything in this world for her to be able to come back. Even if someone had the power to say, "Susie can come back to life but only if it's during that fight she was having with Tig a decade ago," I knew our phone call would be full only of "I love you's" and "I'm sorry's." Back then, it was impossible to understand that our phone call should have been *only* that. When you think you have all the time in the world, hanging up on a loved one seems fine, something to fix later.

Almost exactly a year earlier, I'd had a moment in

which I really understood that life was moving on, and I decided to make more of a concerted effort to start mending my relationship with my mother. For most of my life, my mother had been on a roller coaster of quitting drinking and then starting again. When she admitted she'd started again, she'd explain that it was to dull the pain from her car accident in Colorado. However, it was her habit of hiding her drinking that was crazy-making. Her whole life, there were so many nights when she had supposedly quit and would appear to be drinking coffee out of her morning coffee cup and yet still seem like she'd had quite a few noncaffeinated drinks. She'd be so insistent that it was just coffee that I would begin to believe that maybe she was telling the truth, and I just didn't know what sober looked like. If her drinking was what made her unavailable, her hiding her drinking produced a whole different level of unavailability. I could never answer this question: If all my life she had put such importance on us being close, then why did she let drinking become a wedge that separated us?

I was ready for us to have an open discussion, to acknowledge our problems and make changes. I told her that I was in therapy and that I wanted her to get into therapy so that we could begin working through our issues. I was thrilled when she agreed and found a therapist for both of us in Houston. We went and talked about our general problems, but it didn't feel too productive. My mother wanted to be close but she couldn't do much beyond showing up. She made excuses for everything and tried to distract from the issue while asserting how much she loved me. Trying to work things out with her felt like cornering a wild animal. I could see the therapist looking at her like, "Huh . . . what do I do with this one?"

Ric called me into his office when my mother and I returned and asked about our session. Ric doesn't "believe" in therapy, so it seemed odd that he'd be so interested. I figured he was challenging the situation, and I was eager to let him know that just the fact that my mother went to therapy with me was itself a victory. "I'm happy the session went well," he said, "but sadly you're wasting your time, because unfortunately your mother was recently diagnosed with the very early stages of dementia."

As soon as Ric told me the news, I went into my mother's bedroom, where she was resting, and immediately lay down next to her and began crying while telling her that I loved her. Having no idea that Ric had just told me about her diagnosis, my mother seemed confused about this uncharacteristic outpouring of emotion and sounded shocked as she told me that she loved me, too. She kissed my cheek and held my jaw in her hand. I stayed in bed, and we rested together.

My mother's dementia wasn't full-blown Alzheimer's. But after Ric told me, I recalled moments when she had been repetitive or had missed and confused facts. I would never have thought that something as horrible as dementia could bring any measure of peace to my life, but of all the things that made my mother unavailable, dementia was not something that would push me away. It was an unavailability that I had empathy for, and I knew this the moment I got into that bed and found myself bursting with a compassion that I'd long been struggling to have for my mother. Her not knowing certain things about herself and needing help made her seem vulnerable and childlike, but not childish. For the first time, it was a welcome role reversal.

I made a point to visit her more often and to talk on the phone more regularly. I still felt ready to forgive her for our troubled past, but when I realized that her almost undetectable dementia would likely progress, I had to accept that a large part of our relationship would never be accessible to me again. Since she couldn't contend with my emotions about that relationship, I had no place to put them and so had no choice but to begin the process of letting go. I knew the end was coming. I just didn't know it was coming so soon. And in a way I had never imagined.

My mother's breathing had turned into a consistent gurgle during the last few hours. Twice, I called the nurses in to clear her throat with a suction, before I could accept the fact that clearing her throat was only helping me and not her. She wasn't going to survive no matter what was done. It sounded and felt like she was drowning, and though I was holding her hand, I couldn't save her. I spoke on the phone with a couple of different friends. They were compassionate and eager to help me through this brutal journey, but I discovered that trying to get comfort and true understanding from someone who hasn't lost their own mother is like trying to talk about the feeling of falling in love to someone who has never experienced it. It is simply impossible.

In desperate frustration, I called Kyle, a comedian and one of my closest friends. He was out gambling at some mysterious place he always drives to outside of Los Angeles. Kyle lost his father to brain cancer over a decade ago, and it was the specifics he related from his experience that made me feel less alone. In our nearly two-hour conversation, we went from comparing notes on the depths of hell to chatting about the inane day-to-day. We were in the inane—specifically, I was teasing him about being at a casino alone and blowing his money—when suddenly the gurgling stopped. I had been sitting at the foot of my mother's bed and rubbing her feet. I didn't know what I was waiting for now. Were her eyes going to open? Was she going to make a noise of comfort or discomfort? All I could do was look at her intently. Then, almost immediately after she breathed what was to be her last breath, that dark gray liquid seeped out of her mouth.

"I think my mother just died," I told Kyle. I wasn't even crying; I was still waiting for whatever came next. Was this gray liquid the end or would something else happen? Almost immediately, she began to get cold and stiff. I hung up with Kyle and walked out into the hall. There were a few nurses talking behind a kiosk. I stood right outside the door and said to all of them, "I think my mother just died."

5

Letting Go

I spent nearly the whole week between my mother's death and her funeral lying in bed. No more hospitals. No more rides with crazy, drugged-up cabbies. No more confirmations of death, only a constant fear of what seemed to be my own rapidly encroaching demise. Even if I wanted to go tombstone shopping for my mother (and boy, who wouldn't!), I was too sick. With my condition, it seemed like Ric might need to look for a "buy one, get one free" deal somewhere.

I had tested negative for C-diff and was on the highest dose of medication for recovery, but I was not recovering. I still couldn't keep food inside of me, and my body was disappearing. I pictured dying from kidney failure, starvation, or some bacteria eating a big hole through my intestines. I experienced a bizarre closeness to my mother when I thought about the possibility of dying only weeks after her. As many challenges as my mother and I had, we were so connected on a core level that it almost made sense that we would die weeks apart, like a couple that had been together for years and couldn't live without one another. Often, I had felt like my mother and I were the same person. We shared so many of the same sensibilities—from music to humor to how we took in the world. I suspect part of the reason that my mother eventually supported my dropping out of school was that she, too, was a nonconformist. I never felt like an alien to her. She truly got everything I was about and supported whoever I was trying to be, taking a genuine interest in the hardrock records I was listening to and any scraggly, longhaired friends I brought over to the house, claiming they were adorable and that she couldn't wait to get to know them. And there was truly a long line of smelly rocker pals I brought in and out of the house.

My brother and stepfather picked out the tombstone, and I teetered between trusting them and not caring at all what it looked like. Nothing could register as being as important as the actual loss of my mother. Not how her tombstone was engraved. Not whether or not her picture would be on it. Not how big the tombstone would be. I only had two cares in the world: My mother was dead and was I going to live.

The first time I got out of bed with a real purpose was when it was decided that I should pick out my mother's final outfit. Of the three of us, I was the obvious choice for the job, but my mother did not have the daughter who would shine in this moment. My mother had a finely tuned sense of fashion, while I can typically be found wearing an outfit that can be best described as "something covering my body," and a lot of times—lucky for you—I'll wear that outfit for a week straight.

I stood in my mother's walk-in closet, among her rows of clothes and drawers of scarves and belts. After forty-five minutes, I had about five different options. I laid each one out on her bed. I mixed and matched. I tried to figure out what looked most like her style. "Oh, Sweetie, I'd look like an Easter egg in that!" I'd imagine her saying about the ensemble I'd just created. Okay, I'd nix that, but then a moment later, I'd imagine days when she would have taken pride in dressing like an Easter egg. Oh, what to do. My mother loved mix-matching bright-colored skirts, shoes, and belts. Sometimes she'd wear Converse high-tops with different-colored tights and a denim skirt. Other times, she dressed in a very classically beautiful way. I stood in front of her bed, wondering if I should dress my mother casually or more formally. Easter egg or no Easter egg? Sleeves or no sleeves? How do you decide if someone is going to need a sweater for eternity?

My mother's viewing was a couple of days later. Ric, Renaud, and I stood over her closed coffin before people began arriving. We were all in a focused daze, tears running down our cheeks. It is hard to look at your mother's coffin. Just as I'm sure it's hard to look at your wife's coffin. Through tears, Ric said, "Tig, you did an excellent job picking out her clothes." His compliment made me feel really good. I had made a horrible situation a tiny bit better. And my mother did look really great in the outfit I had chosen: a classic black sleeveless dress with a light sweater on top—just to give her a couple of options.

Hours passed, select family members and friends came by, and I was still pinching myself. Even though I was standing there and seeing it with my own two eyes, my mother couldn't possibly be dead. Every time I told myself, "My mother is dead," or mentioned "my mother's funeral," it felt as foreign and wrong as saying, "My mother is an astronaut." When Beth, my friend for nearly thirty years, walked into the funeral home, I burst into tears. I had told her not to come because she was supposed to be in Austin on vacation, but the moment I saw her, I couldn't believe I had thought I could do this without her. Beth is a solid, strong person who loved my mother dearly, and whom my mother adored. Hugging her felt like grabbing on to a life preserver in the very last moment of struggle.

Although Ric was strongly opposed to the idea, Renaud and I threw a small party for our mother a few days after her funeral. If it hadn't been for Ric's objections, my mother would have had endless get-togethers at the house. The party we threw for her was wonderful but complicated. During it, I felt guilty, devastated, and for short moments, even joyous. We were celebrating her, which made me feel close to her, but at the same time, it seemed like we were almost going behind her back. Deceiving her in some way. All of her favorite people were out by the pool and in our living room; they were eating her favorite food—fish tacos—and listening to her favorite music blaring from her boombox—Willie Nelson, Frank Sinatra, Andy Gibb, Ray Charles, and the song "I Can See Clearly Now" by Johnny Nash. We were having the exact party she always wanted to throw, and she was the one person who wasn't invited. She even missed the part where Ric interrupted the evening with a clinking of his glass and made an emotional toast, saying that he was kicking himself for never having had this party while she was alive to enjoy it.

The day after my mother's party, we drove to her hometown of Pass Christian to bury her. She had requested a small, intimate funeral, so it was very private. But as it turned out, not anonymous, because the moment I walked into the funeral home, a girl who worked there said, "Oh my God, I was just watching you on the TV!" Awesome. I loved getting recognized at my mother's funeral. I must've really hit the big time.

I nervously set up pictures of my mother on tables surrounding her casket. This was supposed to be the official day of honoring her life, and I was ill prepared for everything. I got up to give a small speech and relayed a few funny stories. I was very aware that standing up and talking to people is what I do for a living, and that I was sounding completely scattered and feeling like barely a whisper of a human. I really wanted to talk about how my mother was always behind me and raised me to tell everyone who had a problem with me to "go to hell." But I was in a religious setting, with a priest at my side. Then I realized that if my mother knew I was hesitating, she would have told me to tell the priest to go to hell if he had a problem with it. So, with my mother behind me, covered in a spray of her favorite flowers, yellow roses, I began talking about telling people to go to hell. I told them how my mother told me to tell anyone who hurt my feelings to go to hell; how when people told her to turn her music down, she told them to go to hell; how when a guy cut my mother off while she was driving, he was told to go to hell with an added middle finger. Everyone laughed. Thankfully, even the priest.

Afterward, friends and family met at the yacht club, where they served the typical southern Mississippi gourmet dish: gumbo and fried catfish. We were in the middle of a week of thunderstorms, and this day was forecast to be just as stormy and rainy as the rest, but it turned out to be unbelievably clear with blue skies and a cool breeze coming in off the coast. It was a bright, bright, sunshiny day, and I was standing on the club deck, overlooking the harbor. The only thing missing was my mother. She would have been leaning against the railing, deeply inhaling the air and shouting, "Oh, man, look at that water!" to no one in particular.

During our six-hour drive back to Texas, an unbearable pain spread across the sides of my back. By the time we arrived in Houston, I had to go immediately to the emergency room, where I learned I had a kidney infection. I felt so fragile. I had been out in the world, walking around, crying, giving a eulogy, finally wearing clothes that weren't pajamas, and now I was back in the hospital. I was released after a couple hours and given antibiotics, which put me on edge, since they had originally triggered my C-diff. I tried to negotiate with the doctor, but was told I had no other choice.

When I finally returned to my mother's house, I wanted to crawl into bed and stay there. On my way to my bedroom, I passed a stack of mail Ric had brought in and noticed something from the hospital, addressed to my mother. This struck me as odd since she had just died there. I mean, I know I would have loved to have kept in touch with her, too, but what could the hospital possibly need from my mother now?

Turns out they had a questionnaire for her to fill out:

1. How was your stay at the hospital? Were you satisfied? *Or, did things not go so well?*

2. Did doctors talk in front of you as if you weren't there? *You know, as if you were experiencing heavy brain hemorrhaging and were completely unconscious and on life support? Is that how they were talking in front of you?*

3. During this hospital stay, how often did nurses explain things in a way you could understand? *I mean, considering you had zero brain activity?*

4. During this hospital stay, was the area around your room quiet at night? *Or, could you hear the twelve hours of your daughter, alone at your bedside, sobbing and telling you things she wished she had been brave enough to tell you when you were conscious?*

5. After you left the hospital, did you go directly to your own home, to someone else's home, or to another health facility? *Or directly into the ground in a casket that your family had to pick out last minute because nobody had planned on you tripping on an end table, hitting your head, being put on life support, and dying a day later?*

6. Suggestions for improvement? *Such as, should we stop sending questionnaires to dead people? Or, do you think some dead mother's child needs to find humor in the utmost sadness, considering she's a comedian and it's the first time in her life that everything seemed to disappear and nothing was left to joke about, nothing was funny at all?*

I was furious and wanted to call the hospital and see who was in charge of mailing questionnaires to dead people. But I didn't have the energy. Next to the stack of mail were some cut flowers my mother had arranged in a vase. She had just been here. And she should be sitting right over there in her favorite chair, where she'd spent her last moments of consciousness, reading travel and fashion magazines. That wingbacked chair had been haunting me since I'd come to my mother's house. I'd stare at it from across the room, like, "Oh, it's you." The chair was, of course, an innocent bystander, but it felt complicit in my mother's demise. I knew I could never see it the same again.

Several days after her funeral, I made the decision to sit in the chair. I walked over to it with a silent, careful approach, as if I might find clues that would make me feel better about something that I already knew ended up terribly. Her blood was on the arm. Seeing blood always makes me turn away and clutch my stomach, and yet I found myself moving closer. I removed the cushion, looking for more blood, or for anything that she'd touched. Food. Coins. A nail file. If there had been a half-eaten Triscuit under the cushion, how could she not be alive? Somebody had to have eaten the other half. And explain

the perfectly good nickel wedged in there. I put the cushion back and sat down, totally unsure of what it would
feel like, as if I'd never sat in a chair. My first thought was
that if my mother were alive, I wouldn't be sitting here.
It was her chair. I waited to feel uncomfortable, angry, or
scared, but oddly, I felt close to her again, as though I was
wearing her jacket. Thinking that this was my mother's
blood and that blood signifies life, I rested my arm on the
stain.

A week later, Delza, the housekeeper, arrived to clean
a house that certainly hadn't had time to messy itself with
me in bed, my mother dead, Renaud back in Colorado,
Ric's limited movement, and Bunny's one misplaced toy. I
walked into the kitchen for a glass of water and saw Delza
walking from room to room sobbing, "Miss Susie . . .
Miss Susie . . ." as she dusted shelves and swept floors. It
was clear that I hadn't caught Delza in a freak sob session,
but that this had been going on for a while and was showing no signs of letting up. Delza eventually made her way
into the kitchen, where I had been preparing a smoothie.
Tearfully and in broken English, she told me that my
mother had told her she considered her a sister and that
whenever she liked what my mother was wearing, my
mother gave it to her. This brought me to tears. Before

my mother died, there wasn't a scenario I could imagine where I would have my arms wrapped around my mother's housekeeper as we cried on each other's shoulders. It was awkward. I had never talked to this person except for a meek "hi" in passing, and now we needed each other.

I'd known that my mother loved Delza, but I'd never considered the depth of their bond. I decided to let Delza take a few of my mother's things. She went through my mother's closet piece by piece, crying and remembering which skirt and jacket were my mother's favorites. As she walked out of the house at the end of the day, I saw my mother's ballet slippers on top of a stack of my mother's clothes. My mother had been a ballerina her whole life and had danced all around the house in those shoes, posing in different positions while she did the dishes or cooked. Those ballet slippers were the one thing I couldn't part with, but I didn't know how to express this to Delza, in English or in Spanish. Or even really to myself. I'd never been so focused and emotional over ballet slippers.

When I was four, my mother enrolled me in ballet. A couple months into classes, I had a version of the epiphany I would later have at seventeen, right before I walked out of my high school's front doors for good: I was doing something I didn't want to do all because it was expected

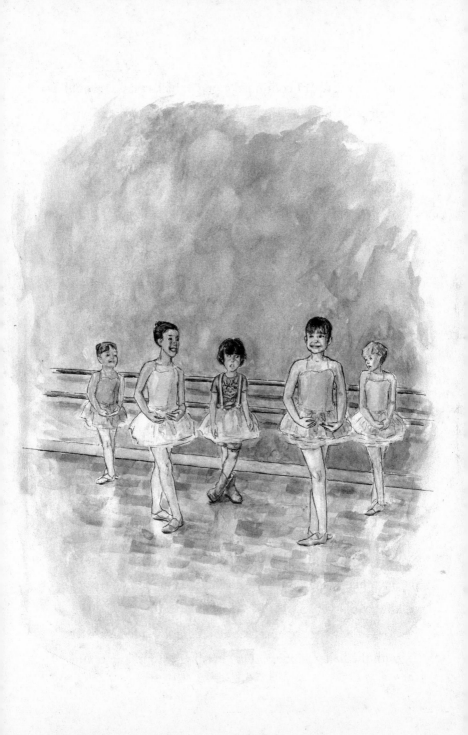

of me. Why? If I continued going to ballet class, I would be living a lie. The only part of ballet that resonated with me was the moment at the end of class when our teacher made us stand in a circle with our little hands cupped behind our backs, ready to receive our surprise: a Tootsie Roll or a peppermint. Oooh, which one will it be?! This was all I went to class for. "Please," I thought during horribly performed plié after horribly performed plié, "can we just cut out this middleman in a tutu, and for the love of God, could someone just give me a Tootsie Roll?"

When our teacher suddenly, inexplicably, stopped giving us candy—were we that bad?—I quit. It was the first time that I had veered away from my mother and begun to pursue my own identity. And for good reason: Why would anyone put themselves through the hell of ballet if no one placed a piece of candy in their hand at the end of class? Of course, I could have just gone out and gotten candy without wearing a tutu. The fact is, when you're a kid, Tootsie Rolls just appear in your general vicinity. You don't have to put a tutu on. You just have to be awake, if that. But I wasn't smart enough to figure any of that out yet.

I didn't want to hurt Delza's feelings, so I let her leave with the ballet slippers. That evening, I found an online program that translates English to Spanish and typed a letter explaining that I was sorry, but that those ballet slippers meant a lot to me because my mother had danced in them for years, and I wanted to keep them. I printed the letter out and, full of dread and anxiety, gave it to Delza the following Friday. I hated the thought of embarrassing her, and the language barrier made it difficult not to embarrass us both. Somehow, I believed my broken English was a version of Spanish that she could understand. She stared at me with true pity as I struggled to explain why I had gone from tearfully hugging her to formally presenting her with a typed document. "Have something to ask you . . . didn't know how," I said. "Got computer. Wanted to translate. Decided to print out letter. Me Tarzan, you Jane." At this point, neither of us had any idea what I was attempting to say, so she read the letter. After some time, she looked up and hugged me and said that of course I could have the slippers back.

Once I had the slippers back, I thought, "Okay, now what? And especially now what if my own life is possibly in question. Hold on to these slippers for the next two months?" Two months, possibly three, was how long I thought I would live. There was also a part of me that had not fully accepted that any of this had actually happened to me, and I began to feel guilty for spending so much time in bed. My life was previously very busy, and I had to constantly remind myself, "Wait, your mother just died and you're, at most, one hundred pounds and dying. You probably don't need to be keeping a tight schedule right now."

I joked about dying because actually saying, "I'm dying," sounded a little dramatic and would have been hard for others to comprehend since I had been discharged from the hospital and the new antibiotics for my kidney infection seemed to be doing their job without reawakening the C-diff. But I really was dying. My body was unable to absorb nutrients. Alone in my bedroom in Spring, Texas, I watched my skeleton emerge. First, my rib cage, then the sharp points of my pelvis, then the lines of my jaw, the peaks of my shoulders. My underwear was baggy, and if I didn't hold on to my belt loop, my pants dropped to the floor.

Each morning, I went to my mother's bathroom, stood in front of her counter with all her bottles of fancy, sweet-smelling lotions, and stared at my diminishing reflection. Then I stepped onto her digital scale. The scale measured weight to the ounce, and each day I saw that I weighed about a half pound less than the day before and was seized with panic. One morning, I calculated that if nothing changed—and I had no reason to believe it would—in two weeks, I would weigh ninety pounds.

Good thing someone from the future didn't tap me on my shoulder and whisper, "I know this appears to be rock bottom, but you're actually only halfway there."

The six weeks I spent at my mother's house trying to recover from C-diff were the loneliest I'd experienced in my life. Friends texted to see how I was doing and each time I found it impossible to convey how grave my condition was. Everyone meant well when they wondered: How are you feeling? How's it going? Do you need anything? Normally, I feel I'm good at communicating and can get my point across clearly, but what I needed could not be expressed in the language of a text. Texting is for small talk, and nothing I was experiencing was small. Nothing I needed could be expected of a friend. Even my doctors couldn't give me what I needed. I needed miracles or magic—two things I didn't even believe in.

Once again, I was in a situation I had never been in, needing comfort from people who could intimately relate—and no one related to C-diff. It is not a widely known disease. Not only had people not experienced what I'd had, but they did not comprehend it. They responded with something like "Oh, that sucks. Yeah, my ex has IBS."

"Lucky dog," I'd think. "What I'd give to have IBS." Eventually, I began saying, "If I had cancer, everyone would instantly know the gravity of my situation."

Oh, the power of suggestion.

A week after the funeral, I decided to go to my mother's dermatologist to get checked for a type of cancer I wouldn't end up having. Mostly, I went because I was sick, and when you're as sick as I was, your full attention goes to every nuance of your body: "Okay, so my entire GI tract is useless. I wonder if my moles are doing what they're supposed to be doing, whatever it is that moles do." Also, it was another opportunity to feel connected to my mother, to be near someone who had known her.

My mother had a great rapport with all of her doctors, but she got along especially well with her dermatologist, Dr. Schmidt. It had been probably thirty years since I had been in his waiting room, flipping through magazines while my mother had her appointment. Now I could read articles and not just look at the pictures, but all I was able to do was mindlessly flip through pages while wondering if I should tell him my mother died or try to remain anonymous. When I was called in, it was clear he didn't recognize me, and my mother and I didn't have the same last name. At the end of the appointment, I told him I was Tig, Susie Cusack's daughter. He jumped back, very surprised and excited, and immediately asked how my mother was doing. He was wearing square Elton John–esque glasses, and I looked at his eyes, knowing I was about to see them change. I carefully told him she had just died after a fall. He gasped while holding his hand over his heart, then crouched down by his sink, saying, "Oh my God, no!" I had honestly been expecting a controlled "I'm so sorry" but I was witnessing what seemed like someone hearing that their favorite person was dead. He apologized for how hard he was taking everything and explained how much he loved my mother and how much she had made him laugh over the years. His reaction overwhelmed my need for comfort, and I found myself thinking I should console him, but all I could do was sit on the exam table and look down at his uncontainable grief. I couldn't even share my tears. I had often noticed that there isn't room for two people to sob, that when one person's crying is interrupted by the start of another's, it almost always severs the line to the original crybaby's emotions.

I was certain my next doctor's appointment wouldn't be as emotional. I was going in for a colonoscopy. There were no doctors who knew my mother at this office, and I would be unconscious for the procedure. When I felt the intense burning pain of the anesthesia running through my veins, I lost consciousness thinking only about getting healthy again. Then I woke up sobbing. Several nurses gathered around, asking what was wrong. They clearly thought it was something medical. I began to hyperventilate, and when I could finally pull myself together, I said, "I'm sorry, I just remembered that my mother died a few days ago."

My mother's death was a recurring nightmare. I could go down one hallway, and everything would be fine. Then I could turn a corner and come across a memory of her, a reminder that she was gone, and it would all start over again. The refrigerator was empty without her fruits and vegetables and bowls of grains she referred to as her "rabbit food." The living room was silent in the early evening when she should have been making loud calls to our cousins the Raffertys, back in Mississippi. The water and food bowls in the yard were all dry. I wondered if her little squirrel, armadillo, and bird friends knew she was gone.

Every time people called the house for her, mostly telemarketers and a few stragglers who didn't know about her death, I had to tell someone else she was dead. Childhood friends came over to see me, and without my mother's doting affections—"Oh, Sweetie, I love how you did your hair!"; "Oh, look at you . . . that shirt's so cute!"—there was a palpable emptiness. The more expressive extension of myself was gone. I tried to tell myself in every possible way that my mother had died, hoping I could begin to get comfortable with the information. I thought about it. I said it out loud. I typed it in e-mails to friends. Every time the news broke, even in my thoughts, my breath would catch in my throat as though I was hearing it for the very first time.

As I write this book, just a few years after her death, I am still hit with sudden waves of understanding that she's gone, followed by deep, deep sadness. This can happen anywhere, and I am often not alone when it does. I can be out to dinner with friends or live onstage and telling jokes and then it slams into me: *My mother died*. I get tripped up for a second, and there is something very appealing about letting that cold thought wash me away to numbness, but I move through, back into my unwanted reality. I picture my mother watching me getting thrown by her permanent absence. I know she would always want me to be happy, but I also have to think she would be pleased on some level to know how much a part of me she was, that missing her stopped me in my tracks.

Even though I thought I was probably going to die at my mother's house, I felt determined to perform in a live stage show for Ira Glass's radio show, *This American Life*. When the show was planned nine months earlier, it had seemed unlikely for the very different reason that it was an unreal opportunity. It was during the fourth week at my mother's house that I called Ira to let him know that I was losing half a pound a day and didn't know what kind of condition I was going to be in when I got to New York City in two weeks to perform. My scheduled performance for *This American Life* was my life's only bright spot, shining just a little off in the distance. Ira encouraged me to drop out of the show and focus on my health, assuring me that I could do another show in the future. Fairly certain that I didn't have a future, I told him that I would be there in a couple of weeks—no matter what shape I was in.

Things had gotten pretty desperate by this point. I was light-headed and hungry most of the time, looking at food I wanted to eat but couldn't, while more of my skeleton appeared—my breastbone and the long bones in my arms. Since the pills and food my medical doctors were recommending were obviously not working, my girlfriend, Brooke, decided I needed to try something completely different and contacted her nutritionist. I carefully followed the nutritionist's every suggestion, each day taking a refrigerated probiotic capsule, powdered vitamin C, powdered amino acids, and a powdered meal replacement mixed with water.

Within an hour, I noticed I wasn't running off to the bathroom or feeling sick to my stomach. It was the first time in two months that my body wasn't totally rejecting my suggestions. I felt like we were a team again.

Sharp pains still shot through my gut, but within a couple of days, I stopped losing weight. I felt electrified. In the action movie of my life, I had fallen off a building and somehow I had managed to grip a ledge. I didn't know how I was going to get out of this situation, but at least I wasn't falling anymore. I had a finger grip on survival while my pajamas with little pigs flying all over them slid off my bony limbs.

My fifth week at my mother's I was finally healthy enough to leave for New York. Packing my little suitcase felt like starting all over again. I was anxious and excited to be well enough to leave the house, yet terrified of my fragility. What if I slipped up and took a bite of a muffin before I was completely ready? A gust of wind could even be a problem. And couldn't I get really sick again? What if I discovered I wasn't funny anymore? What if I could never work to support myself again? What would I do?

Still, it was exciting to think that life might actually continue, even without my mother. I bought a ticket to New York with my body weighed down by several very substantial new pounds and the thought that this had better be an *explosively great* show. After everything I'd been through, I wasn't in the mood to hear people leaving saying, "Yeah, it was a pretty fun show" or "I've heard her tell that story before."

When I left for New York, Ric was out meeting with an estate attorney. I felt extra bad that I happened to be leaving on this day, since it would have been his and my mother's thirty-seventh wedding anniversary, a day he would've been taking her out to eat at Perry's to have lobster, her favorite meal. It felt extremely inadequate, but I left a good-bye note and a large bouquet of yellow roses on the coffee table.

6

Diagnosis

There was no monumental day when I discovered the lump in my breast. There was only the day I was with Brooke and felt a lump on my left breast that I vaguely remembered feeling about two years earlier but had thought nothing of. I mean, did I feel one then? Perhaps. And as I felt that lump I felt another one, on the right breast, which I also remembered feeling before and finding not as pronounced and even impossible to find on some days. Because of this, and because the lumps on each breast were nearly symmetrical, each on the outside, I believed everything was normal. I considered myself a healthy person. I decided that my lumpy breast tissue was merely the result of the ebb and flow of hormones.

Brooke, however, believed I needed to get it checked out immediately. Instead of making a doctor's appointment, I spent the next couple months teasing Brooke by removing my shirt and saying, "Hey, wanna touch my cancer?" It was really fun to walk past her holding my chest and blurting out, "Ow! My cancer!" And then, completely unrelated—as in, we did not connect this to my "benign" lumps—Brooke one day changed the words to the chorus of a popular Martina McBride song that seemed to be playing all the time on our local country music station. The song, "I'm Going to Love You Through It," is about a man supporting his wife who has been diagnosed with breast cancer, and instead of singing, "Just take my hand, together we can do it, / I'm gonna love you through it," Brooke sang: "Just take my hand, together we can do it / Your tits have cancer." It cracked me up, it cracked her up. It was just ridiculousness. Neither of us stopped after "Ha ha your tits have cancer" to think, "Hmm . . . here are these lumps . . . I wonder if these *particular* tits *do* have cancer."

Five months after I'd really noticed the lump on my left breast and almost two months after my C-diff and my mother's death, I returned to L.A. having just recorded *This American Life*. My health was seemingly on the mend, but my relationship was now on its deathbed. Brooke had understandably become impatient with the hell that my life had become, and I had become impatient with her asking how I was doing since my answer was always "not good" or "getting worse." By the time I'd begun snapping, "If I get any better, I'll let you know!" I didn't believe we were actually in love or had enough of a foundation to stabilize the relationship through these tough times. This vicious tension seemed to be a sign not only that our connection lacked depth but that we were trying to break up without verbalizing it. I soon reached the point at which I was even yelling at her to please leave me and go be with someone else. If she left me, I wouldn't feel guilty—another negative emotion I didn't have the capacity to handle at the time.

In order to get perspective on our muddled feelings, we decided to take a couple week-long breaks from our relationship, but I was unable to get the clarity I needed when Brooke continued to contact me. After the unsuccessful attempts at taking space from each other, we made an appointment with a therapist. While driving to my apartment, I asked her what she wanted to talk about in our therapy session, and she said, "Everything." "Oh my God," I thought, "I can't do this." I was certain that trying to mend our relationship would be yet another way I might find myself miserably dangling in purgatory. I desperately needed stability since so many things I'd assumed were concrete, or at least, here for the foreseeable future, had simply and quickly vanished. It became beyond apparent to me that we just needed to break up. Right then. By the time she dropped me off at my loft downtown, I was single and not quite ready to mingle.

Three months after Brooke had told me that I needed to get my breasts examined immediately, I went to the doctor's for a follow-up checkup for C-diff and told the internist that I also had this lump on my left breast (the one on the right was so small and hard to locate I didn't even mention it). I said it like "Hey, I also have this tooth that's been kind of sensitive when I chew gum." She examined me, felt what I was talking about, and suggested that since I was forty-one, I might as well get my first mammogram.

Three weeks after that, I went in for my mammogram feeling I was being quite thorough in my preventive care. When the doctor said she'd call with the results, I didn't feel as though I was waiting to hear if I had cancer. I felt as if I was waiting to hear I didn't have cancer. I forgot about the mammogram and went on with my life. Why wouldn't I? No one that I knew of in my family had ever had breast cancer. I had quit smoking when I was twenty-five years old. Sure, I had started when I was eight, but I was still relatively healthy and young. And most of all, as insane as it may sound, I really thought because my breasts were so small, my likelihood of getting breast cancer was the same as a man's: very slim, just like my teats.

I still had zero concern when my doctor's office called to tell me I needed to come in to the cancer center for further diagnostic testing because my mammogram was abnormal. I'd heard from my doctor, and many other people, that abnormal mammograms that turn out to be benign are quite common. I brought Sascha, the ex-girlfriend who'd talked me onto the plane, because she wanted to be there for me when I got out of testing. She wandered into a nearby mall while I was poked and prodded. Put in gown after gown. Bed after bed. Machine after machine. What was supposed to be a quick forty-five-minute process turned into nearly five hours. I was told I could go get lunch, and met Sascha at a nearby deli. No part of me felt like I was waiting to hear anything other than: "Just as we suspected, it was an abnormal mammogram. How was that sandwich for ya?" I did not have cancer. There was no way the chorus of my life was going to be changed to: "Your tits have cancer / Who knows who's going to love you through it?"

At the end of my fourth hour at the cancer center, the

doctor entered my room and asked, "How are you?" I said I was fine, but she was too cautious, and I was suddenly paranoid and wishing there was someone else in the room to help me gauge her tone. She gently told me that they'd seen the lump that I'd come in for on the left breast and that they'd also found one on the right. I couldn't figure out if what I was hearing was scary. Was I being told I had cancer? If I completely freaked out like I wanted to, would I be overreacting? Would someone else hear all this and say, "Oh, Tig, you don't have cancer. She's a doctor and she has to say things like that." I felt my brow furrow and heard myself ask if she was concerned. "Yes," she said. "Actually, I am."

"Wait, are you telling me there's a chance I have cancer?" I asked, thinking that possibly they had the wrong information. Like maybe they had gotten my files mixed up with someone else's. And besides that, my mother had just died, I had recently split with my girlfriend, and I had been in the hospital for C-diff. I was the single most unlikely person to have another bad straw piled onto the camel's back. I'm not a superstitious person, but I was beginning to believe that I was on a bad streak and that life had made a decision to take me down.

Ira Glass soon set me straight on this point, reassuring me that everything happening to me only represented true randomness; that people think "random" means scattered when, in fact, randomness *can* look like a pattern. To prove his point, he told me that when the episode of *This American Life* that I appeared on was projected live into theaters around the world, and a raffle with two prizes for the entire viewing audience was offered, both winners were seated in the same small theater. And that, same as my back-to-back hardships, was truly random.

But lying down in the patient room at the cancer center that day, I didn't feel like I was living in a random universe. I felt cursed. How quickly I had gone from always being annoyingly lucky in the eyes of my friends—having "Tig Luck"—to being pitied and feeling pathetic. I was no longer walking out of a comedy club and stepping on five one-hundred-dollar bills on the pavement beneath my car door. Gone were the days of deciding what I really wanted was an outdoor cat and coming home to find a ratty little thing with a sweet meow and bent tail curled up on an oil spot in my driveway.

The doctor said she couldn't confirm anything without biopsies, but based on everything she'd seen today, it was quite probable that I did have cancer. She asked if I had any questions. I didn't really react. I felt like I had just been told I had cancer but also like I had not been told that I had cancer. Here I was again: dangling in purgatory.

When I'd learned my mother had fallen and was not going to make it, I couldn't fathom driving to the airport, taking my shoes off for security, boarding a plane, and then spending several hours strapped to a chair while hurtling through the sky. I wanted to be teleported. I had that same feeling right in this moment. My skeleton had been removed, and all hundred or so pounds that I'd become were collapsing under the gravity of reality. The tedium of traveling anywhere, even the short drive back to my apartment, seemed utterly impossible. Then I realized I didn't just need to get myself home, I still had to get Sascha home, which meant merging with five o'clock traffic and heading in the exact opposite direction of my apartment, deep into the Valley.

We drove very silently and slowly toward the Valley. Sascha wanted to be with me, comfort me, and come home with me, but I declined. There wasn't a single human being in my life who I wanted to be around. I didn't want to be comforted by my most recent ex-girlfriends or my newest romantic interest. There was nothing I needed someone to say. I felt so alone, which only made me want to be alone. I didn't want a hug. I wasn't hungry. I was nothing. I couldn't even cry.

When I finally pulled into my parking spot outside my apartment, I just sat there and exhaled, staring through the windshield. I imagined the aerial view of myself as a red target focused on the top of my car, as if there was a helicopter searching for lonely people with bad news. It would follow me as I walked into my apartment, and perhaps for the next several months. "What an odd job those pilots would have," I thought, and then decided walking into my apartment and riding the elevator just shy of ten floors was something I needed to put off for a while.

The hour and a half I spent alone after dropping Sascha off and driving home had allowed me time to want to finally reach out to someone, so I called my manager, Hunter. Hunter only has four clients, and not to be braggadocious, but it's a pretty safe assumption that I might be in his top three. I felt like a parent telling their kid that the person he depended upon was possibly not going to be around for much longer, that because I wasn't sure I was going to be okay, he couldn't be sure he was going to be okay. I know Hunter's well-being wasn't his concern in that moment, but it was mine. I'd been his client for over four years at that point, and we talked several times a day. He's heard all about my romantic relationships, he's visited me in the hospital, and he's helped me move—all for just 10 percent of my income. And now he was hearing that I probably had cancer. Hunter was silent for a few seconds and then his voice cracked as he asked me to keep him updated on what the doctors said. We spoke for a little longer and then got off the phone because neither one of us wanted to break down in front of the other. After hanging up, I sat in my car and finally cried.

The moment I walked into my apartment, there was a magnetic pull that forced me into my bed. I stared at my ceiling with only two thoughts: "There's no way I have cancer" and "Oh my God, I have cancer and I'm going to die."

When I'd left the doctor's office, the doctor had tried to get me to schedule a biopsy, and I told her I had to record my podcast, *Professor Blastoff*, the following day and that I'd get back to her. I'm sure she hoped that when I got back to her I'd also let her know what exactly a podcast was. So, indeed, the day after my appointment, instead of going in for a biopsy or taking ten minutes to schedule one, I crawled out of bed and went to the studio to make sure ridiculous jibber jabber between comedian friends could be recorded and downloaded for free around the world.

People around me didn't understand my unwillingness to move forward. They thought I needed to be proactive, and I thought they should have their mothers die and go through a breakup and be days away from a possible cancer diagnosis and see how quickly they drive to get their chest skewered repeatedly with what looked like a ten-inch ice pick so they can find out if they have yet another potentially deadly disease. I imagined they might also do what I did, which was stay under the blankets in their baggy underwear and imagine the worst.

On my fourth day home from the cancer center, I managed to stop examining my bedroom ceiling and submit myself to examining the doctors examining the tiny bloody chunks they were slowly pulling out of my tumors with their long, sharp tools and placing in a petri dish next to my face.

Ahhhhhh . . . heaven.

I left the biopsies feeling like I had been in a serious car crash, and I was supposed to appear on *Conan* the following night and then leave for a week-long run of shows at the Montreal Just for Laughs comedy festival. I had stubbornly not canceled these because I had wanted to believe that if I kept going through life like everything was normal, then it finally would be. I called Hunter and told him to cancel everything because I couldn't move my body. Instead of an impressive tour schedule on my website, I was looking at: Canceled, Canceled, Canceled, Canceled, Canceled, Canceled.

On July 25, 2012, my fifth day home from the cancer

center, I'd finally moved from my bed to my couch when the phone rang. I saw it was the doctor's office and decided this was going to be the call that would put my mind at ease. I would be told that everything was fine, that my rack looked sweet. Instead, I was told that I had cancer in both breasts and that I needed to make an appointment as soon as possible with an oncologist and a surgeon to learn what stage I had and figure out a plan. I hung up the phone, thinking that I was going to die and my mother didn't even know.

I put off meeting with the surgeon and oncologist for nine days. When I finally went, I brought my friend Beth. I've always known her to be nurturing, but not hyperemotional; calm and collected, but not stoic. I always listed Beth as my emergency contact, never imagining there would be an actual emergency. Yet here I was, standing next to my emergency contact, hoping she would comprehend everything and ask the right questions. Which she did, until the surgeon told us that I had stage II cancer in both breasts and that the tumor on the left was invasive. Invasive, as in, the cancer was not contained and might have spread, but they couldn't know where it had spread or how much until they did surgery. I felt my mind float away. Beth didn't ask questions and she didn't move.

She was frozen. We were both hearing information we were simultaneously trying to process and reject.

I don't recall anything else the surgeon said, I only remember wanting to get out of my chair to go curl up in a ball somewhere on the floor of his office, like an animal trying to die. The next thing I remember was standing on the sidewalk and crying with my head pressed into Beth's shoulder while she hugged me. This was truly an emergency contact if ever there was one. My crying, which I don't even do much of privately, turned into sobbing and hyperventilating for all approaching and departing Beverly Center shoppers to see.

Needing my mother to comfort me about her death was an insatiable, unresolvable problem. And now, having cancer without having a mother brought on a similar, and similarly insurmountable, problem: I needed to go home, but I would forever be unable to.

Beth offered to drive me to my apartment, but I wanted to drive alone, saying to myself: "I have cancer. I have cancer. I have cancer. I have cancer. I have cancer. I have cancer. I have cancer. I have cancer. I have cancer. I have cancer."

I called a handful of my closest friends and told them my diagnosis. If I was laser-focused on trying to make sense of the fact that I was now one of those people who had cancer, my friends were trying to make sure that I swiftly became one of those people who didn't have cancer. My e-mail and phone were soon full of messages offering different treatment recommendations, spas, doctors, and diets. I'd always thought of myself as someone who would take a more natural, Eastern medicine route to treat a serious medical condition. But once I heard the words "stage II invasive cancer," holistic medicine seemed at best a preventive measure, and I immediately wanted the Western folks scooping things out of and off of my body.

My friend Stef called her aunt, an ob-gyn in Los Angeles. Stef had studied biological anthropology. With her knowledge of *Homo erectus* and my ability to play guitar and drums, we were sure to get somewhere. She took pages of notes full of words neither of us knew, acronyms that sounded like the names of *Star Wars* action figures, and tons of numbers to call with side notes on who to say recommended me. We compared Stef's notes to Google searches or the notes of my own doctors, and still nothing made sense. It began to feel as though we had asked directions to someplace very important but the signs suggested contradictory routes and many paths were full of roadblocks, detours, and warnings—and should these warnings be ignored, it would put me into a no-turning-back zone.

It seemed I no longer had any casual or lighthearted choices to make. Like, should I wear my Pretenders or my Van Halen T-shirt today? Should I get a kitten in the next couple months? Maybe I'll be vegan this year.

After telling me I had stage II invasive breast cancer, the surgeon had implied a double mastectomy was mandatory for my survival. All I had been prepared to hear was that I needed a lumpectomy. I'd known people who'd had those and they were alive and doing well. No one I knew had a double mastectomy, at least not that I was aware of.

For months now, each new fork in the road seemed to veer off in a drastic direction, with no possible return: Eat a handful of cereal and writhe around in pain for three days, take your mother off life support, break up with your girlfriend, have both of your boobs removed and wait for the PTSD that you were warned might follow. Did I really have to agree to get a double mastectomy? How had my situation become so severe that I had no choice but to permanently change my body in order to live?

I waited several days to tell my brother my news. Since our mother's death, we had been in each other's life on a more regular basis, and I wanted to protect him a little longer from the potentially devastating, life-altering news I had to deliver. When I called him, our mother had only been dead for four months; it seemed like the epitome of "too soon." In a matter-of-fact way, I told him I had breast cancer, assured him that I was learning about it, told him about the advances science has made, and reviewed all the appointments and second and third opinions I had lined up with the help of my many concerned friends. I did not cry. I felt him trying hard to receive the news and react like the strong, big brother he was until his voice started shaking and he began to cry. Then I cried. For the first time, it occurred to me that our mother had birthed for each of us a buddy for life; that even with all the baggage and boundaries that come tangled with adulthood, we would simply always be defenseless children to each other.

Delivering the news to my brother started a constant flow of e-mails, texts, and phone calls. Our continuous contact was a welcome shift, but one I discovered I wasn't completely prepared for. Processing the cancer diagnosis didn't make me chatty, so I really had nothing to say to him—or anyone outside my tight group of friends—until I knew whether or not the cancer had spread farther into my body. Wouldn't I look ridiculous if I had a breakdown in front of everybody and then my doctors told me my condition was not that serious after all? Or did I only have two years to live? Three? How had I gone from never making a guess about how much time I had before I died to doing it twice in a few months for totally different reasons? How was it even possible that there had been a number of days when I'd had pneumonia, C-diff, *and* invasive cancer all at the same time, and didn't even know it? I breathed in and out and read people's e-mails and texts but rarely responded.

The only person I felt I needed to contact and had not yet was my stepfather, Ric. Knowing he would request a lot of information, I waited until I knew as much about my health as possible and until the feeling of delaying the call was worse than actually making it. As I struggled to dial his number, I could immediately appreciate how difficult it must have been for him to dial mine four months before to make the life-has-changed-in-an-irreversibly-horrible-way phone call. Chatting casually at first would have felt like lying, so after I said hello I calmly told him I had bilateral breast cancer and rushed to answer what I thought would be his next question by stating that I was getting treatment as soon as possible. Ric is not effusive, so it was comforting to anticipate nothing more than a monotonous "Tig, that's terrible news. I'm sorry to hear that. Do you have a good doctor?" Instead he gasped and exclaimed, "Oh my God!" in such a vehement way that I quickly understood just how much Ric cared about me and how serious my situation was. His reaction was eerily similar to Dr. Schmidt's on hearing that my mother had died.

I have cancer. I have cancer. I have cancer. I have cancer. I have cancer. I have cancer. I just sat around having cancer and thinking about having cancer all the time. I maybe made room for a few other small thoughts, like "Oh, my bladder's full. I should go empty this thing," but then it was back to having cancer. Fear of dying came in waves as I looked around my house at all of my unused furniture. There were chairs I never sat on, and I wondered why I ever bought them in the first place. I began to have fantasies of taking everything back to the store:

Me: Yes, hi. I'd like to return this.

Employee: The reason?

Me: I have cancer.

Employee: Do you have a receipt?

Me: No, but I do have cancer.

My brain now flipped back and forth between feeling confident that I'd beat cancer and thinking, "Holy God, I have invasive cancer and I better figure out where I want my lonesome tombstone to be standing for an eternity with no visitors." People have such a strong urge to make their mark here on earth, the final one being their tombstone. Whenever I drive past a graveyard, I think of how many tombs are not being visited, and haven't been for decades, except by the lawn-mower guy as he rolls by. It seems like the typical tombstone is really only visited for fifty years, a hundred years, max?

A fresh tombstone gets a lot of visits right away, for sure. On tour a few years ago somewhere in the Midwest, I took a walk around town and found this really cool, old graveyard. I came across what appeared to be a fresh tombstone that had about fifteen balloons tied to it and was surrounded by party hats, kazoos, streamers, a triple-layered cake with burned-out candles, and a sign exclaiming HAPPY BIRTHDAY! I just stood there and stared at the stillness of the party that wasn't going on. At all. No matter how much you dress up a tombstone, there's still nothing happening. I wondered who blew out the candles and if anybody had any sense of humor about it as they blew up the balloons and ordered the cake: "I'd like it to say, 'Lordy, lordy, look who's forty.'" Or, perhaps this was done by a group of sincere people with zero sense of humor who promised "Johnny," who was dying way too young, that they'd always keep celebrating his birthday long after he was gone, and by golly they were sticking to their word. The longer I stared at it, the funnier and more ironic it became. And yes, this is a huge hint to my friends and family for what I'd like for my birthday after I die. Don't sullenly hang out around my tombstone, just dress the thing up in celebration and then take the party elsewhere. Please. Thanks in advance.

7

Largo

Standing on the side of the stage listening to Ed Helms wrap up his set at Largo was the closest I'd come to having stage fright in a long time. I was pacing back and forth, my heart pounding. I had an opening line that I knew was either going to make or break my performance. Ed Helms finished his set, then announced, "Please welcome Tig Notaro!" I walked out, waving into the darkness.

Nine days earlier, I was meant to be doing this very show, my regular *Tig Has Friends at Largo,* when I found out I had cancer and was told I had to make another appointment with an oncologist and a surgeon to learn what stage it was and to get more details. I called the owner of Largo, my longtime friend Mark Flanagan, and told him that I had just been diagnosed with cancer and was in quite a bad place. Instead of canceling the show, he suggested that I move it to the following week. I thought either he hadn't understood what I'd said or he was out of his mind. To humor him, I agreed, with the stipulation that I would be able to cancel the show up until the very last minute if I still wasn't up to it. Flanagan agreed, and I started writing.

I had nine days and took my laptop everywhere I went, meticulously writing down jokes, concepts, and moments I would share onstage. I was not in the habit of writing down my stand-up material. Normally, I had ideas and those ideas became a few words jotted down on scraps of paper and were mostly worked out over time onstage. But I was working under a pressing deadline and the terrifying thought that I might not have much more time, that this might be my last performance.

My goal had been to write a good half hour of new material for my Largo show, and being at rock bottom was turning out to be oddly fruitful. Even when I wanted to spend quality time with friends and not think about cancer, my brain operated like a busy assistant eager to please—constantly buzzing me with ideas for a new punch line or setup. I was more focused and driven than I'd ever been.

I waited two or three days after getting the generic

"hello, you have cancer, good-bye" phone call and then scheduled the next available appointment with my surgeon, which happened to be the day before my Largo show, which meant that I would be performing one day after finding out just how numbered my days might be. I knew I was supposed to be meeting several possible surgeons and oncologists, and researching procedures I might need and even alternatives to Western medicine. I knew I was supposed to be doing *something*, but I still needed to work out how I felt about the sentence "You have cancer" before I could go and find out what, exactly, it was going to mean for me.

Worried friends would inquire if I'd gotten answers, and I'd hear them ask if I'd gotten "cancers." Any bodily pain or discomfort was reason to believe that my cancer was spreading rapidly. I no longer trusted even a raucous sneeze to be something I could just dismiss. Then came the day I walked past my dresser and glanced at my second-grade school picture, which had always blended in with the smattering of loose change and random paper clips. I had thought of the term "inner child" as mumbo-jumbo therapy jargon, but as I stared at my tentative second-grade smile I felt a direct link to that little kid. I saw clearly that this was me: the me that didn't know what I knew now; the me that couldn't imagine what was coming; the me that was pure and healthy; the me who thought I was really nailing it fashion-wise by matching a striped shirt with my slightly differently striped Mork from Ork suspenders. I was looking at the innocent beginning of what was quite possibly coming to an end. In the excited voice someone might use to deliver good news to a child, I picked up the picture and told my seven-year-old self, "You're gonna get *cancer*!"

The day before my show, I went to meet with my surgeon, bringing Beth with me, and learned that my cancer was stage II and invasive and that I needed to schedule surgery immediately. As I stood outside the cancer center crying, Flanagan texted to see if I was still going to do the show. I simply texted "yes," thinking that things were not only not going up, but my life was likely ending, and I needed to perform one last time.

The day of my show, I did what I always did: not prepare. I didn't review my notes from the previous nine days, I just went about my day, totally consumed by the thought of how the show was going to go. The show was billed as my own with unannounced special guests. Anyone in the audience was there specifically to see me. They were most likely anticipating "No Moleste" and my impression of an impersonator. Just ridiculousness. I had none of that for them. I didn't want to share my run-ins with Taylor Dayne, and I couldn't relate to the silliness of hearing some audience members laugh as they said that they were paying to hear three minutes of squeaks and screeches from a wooden stool I was awkwardly pushing around the stage.

I was going to be tossing aside my reliable jokes and winging it not only with new material but improvised material as well—all of it raw and vulnerable, and quite possibly not the least bit funny. I had outlined topics I wanted to touch on, but I still couldn't picture what my opening line would be. I knew I wanted the audience to partly feel as though I was saying something as casual as "A funny thing happened on the way to my oncologist . . ." but I felt torn open and this line of thinking lacked a directness and an honesty that I was anxious to share. I tried to picture myself pulling up the very stool they wished I'd start pushing around the stage and just begin with "Hey, so I've gone through a really rough spot in life recently, and I have some really raw material to run past you . . ." Then I would chat with the audience about my life as if I were chatting with a friend. But every time I pictured myself doing that, I didn't like how I would essentially be apologizing ahead of time for how not-thought-out my stories and jokes were. I didn't want to come across as taking myself too seriously either. I needed to find the happy medium between sharing my situation openly and making light of it. I wanted it to be honest but still be a comedy show. This didn't seem totally impossible; it just seemed more likely that I would get hit by a bus in the crosswalk on the way to my show.

An hour and a half before show time, I got in the shower. This is usually when I start to have vague ideas about what I'm going to do onstage in the next hour or two. I decided that I had to shock the audience into laughter. If I just said, "I have cancer," it would not be funny. As I shampooed my hair, I thought, what if I opened my show with "Hello, how is everyone doing tonight? I have cancer." I burst into a maniacal fit of laughter when I thought about saying this with the same delivery as the trite "Hello, how is everyone doing tonight? Any birthdays? Anyone celebrating anything? Who's drinking tonight?" I was laughing so hard I couldn't help but wonder if this was what insanity felt like. I felt light as a feather—which I pretty much was—and intoxicated. I felt certain this was the only way to force the audience to process the bad news and then take a leap and catch up to the point that had taken me nine days to arrive at, the point where there was a way to laugh about something so unfunny. Then I thought, "No way, I can't do any of this. What if I offend someone in the audience who has cancer or knows someone with cancer?"

And then it dawned on me: "Oh yeah—I have cancer. Me. I do." Still, I wasn't sure I should do it.

I don't laugh too easily. Even when I begin to piece together something amusing that I want to try out on-stage, my own reaction ranges narrowly from a tilt of the head to a slight smirk accompanied by the thought "Hmm, that's funny." To get me genuinely laughing, I need to find something utterly absurd. And this opening Largo line had the perfect combination of silliness and reality with a curve ball.

It was beginning to make me laugh harder than the time my friend Kyle and I spotted Santa Claus in the parking lot of a McDonald's in Encino. We had been working on a comedic Christmas video and were becoming increasingly frustrated as we searched every Santa-for-hire website for the perfect-looking Santa. Kyle wanted to take a break and treat himself to a couple of burgers at McDonald's, which he insisted on eating in his car in their parking lot. As soon as we parked, we saw a woman in the distance who was acting so insane that Kyle began to videotape her on his cell phone. Possibly half a second after he pressed record, our view was interrupted by a big white Cadillac driving past us. The man behind the wheel slowly turned and looked our way, and by golly it was Santa Claus. The exact specimen we had been searching for all afternoon. I pointed at the Cadillac and cried, "Oh my God, Kyle, it's Santa Claus!"

"Oh my God," Kyle yelled, "do you think he'll talk to us?!" We peeled out of the parking lot and started chasing Santa Claus down Ventura Boulevard. When we pulled up next to him at a light, I realized I hadn't figured out what I was going to say once we caught him. I rolled down my window and awkwardly said, "Hi ... You know who you look like, right?"

"Santa Claus," he said matter-of-factly. I explained that my friend and I wanted to hire him to play Santa Claus in a video we were making. I left off some details like that we would be filming him taking a bubble bath with one of Kyle's childlike characters, who would not know that this particular Santa Claus was perverted. He reached a hand out of his car window and gave me his business card. When he drove off, I read his e-mail address, which was his name @ some very conservative church.org. I turned to Kyle and said, "Oh man, this guy is not going to take a bubble bath with you."

Driving back to Kyle's, I thought about the video we just took and realized we had quite possibly captured the most ridiculous moment in the history of human beings alive on this planet. I asked Kyle to pull over and play back the video so I could show him that this was the case. He began to think about what I had just said, and we both began snorting and crying, all hunched over, laughing so hard that we became ugly people. And we still hadn't even seen the video. Kyle finally pulled over and pressed play. The crazy woman is a speck in the distance for a brief moment, and then a boat of a car slowly drives past and the driver looks in our direction and you hear me earnestly shout, "Oh my God, Kyle, it's Santa Claus!" My excited finger darts into the frame, pointing, and you hear Kyle, a full-grown man, yell at the top of his lungs, "Oh my God, do you think he'll talk to us?!" If someone came across this video with zero backstory, it would truly appear as though two adult buffoons thought that they saw Santa Claus driving an old Cadillac through a McDonald's parking lot in the middle of a hot summer day in Encino.

Who would have thought that the next time I'd be

laughing that hard, I would be on the brink of announcing to hundreds of people that I had cancer? I sure didn't.

When I got to Largo, comedians Mary Lynn Rajskub, Ed Helms, and Bill Burr were there. We all chatted briefly backstage, but I could feel myself withholding. Acting. None of them knew that I was harboring this huge secret or knew anything about my last few months. Mary Lynn was up first, then Ed. They both were having solid sets. I didn't have the confidence that my set could open or close the show, so I figured I'd wedge myself right in the middle, before Bill and then Louis C.K., who was arriving later and would close out the night. If my set bombed, I had two of the strongest comedians following me to make everyone feel like they got their money's worth. I sat backstage, picturing people as they left saying, "That was the most uncomfortable thing I have ever witnessed. Good thing Bill Burr was there." Or, maybe a year from now, someone would be saying, "Remember when Tig Notaro told the audience that she had cancer and her mother had died?" And their friend would make a face like they were smelling a waft of rancidness, then close their eyes while nodding their head and saying, "Yes, I unfortunately do."

Even though I knew there was no way for me to truly

understand what it would be like to hear what I was about to reveal or anticipate how I would feel saying it, I did know that there was no way I could start crying. I needed the audience to be empathetic but open, not overwhelmed and shut down by sorrow and pity.

Ed wrapped up his set and introduced me. Oh my gosh, here we go. I had never before been scared of my material and simultaneously electrified by it. I felt like a live wire. The crowd cheered. Dammit. I could feel myself about to cry.

"Hello. Good evening. Hello. I have cancer, how are you," I said, my voice trembling as the crowd's excited laughter told me they didn't get it. I continued, my voice still trembling, "Hi, how are you? Is everyone having a good time? I have cancer." I felt like we were all standing on a bridge that only I knew was going to collapse. Some people kept laughing, eagerly waiting for the punch line, while others' laughter became confused and hesitant, like "Wait . . . what is this, some kind of a joke?"

Within moments, I could see some people in the first few rows crying, holding their hands over their chests, or shaking their heads. I saw one girl grab her face and mouth "No, no, no" over and over again. Soon I knew every single person had realized, *Oh, she really does have cancer.*

Now it was my job as a comedian to get every silenced, stunned person back to laughing. I would go deep with the truth of what had been happening, even in a joke, and when the room got quiet, or I heard a lot of "ohhhhs," I made it my mission to yank everyone out of the dark hole by delivering a lighter joke or asking why they were taking this so hard—which caused the laughter that we all needed.

Within the first couple minutes, the show was going much better than I had ever imagined. I was truly shocked because the change in my routine felt as dramatic as it would have if I had suddenly shifted into doing racist shock material. But when I knew the audience really understood I had cancer and was still laughing, I began to feel confident that whatever I said, the audience members were going along for the ride and were the exact, perfect people to support me through it. My jokes about my lumps, my last moments next to my mother in her last moments, and my frustrations with the idea of a God who piles it on heavy were not just received well—I felt thoroughly heard and embraced. No one was on autopilot with faint smiles on their faces, waiting to laugh because they were at a comedy show. Everyone, including me, was living moment to

moment, processing raw truths in the dark. It was exhilarating and freeing. I still had cancer, but I felt em-
powered, as though I had an edge over the competition.
My joy and determination had me one up at this point. I
almost cried three different times: the moment I walked
out onstage; when I half jokingly suggested I stop my
performance to avoid bumming people out and a guy
yelled out, "This is fucking amazing!"; and then when I
got a standing ovation.

Halfway through my show, I took a beat, realizing
that this was a really special moment in my life that would
never come again. I was thankful that, on a whim, I had
remembered to ask Flanagan to record it. I honestly
thought I was just sharing my most personal thoughts
with three hundred or so people and that maybe, slowly
over time, word would get out, and if I lived, a few years
down the road, a comic friend would come up to me and
say, "Hey, I heard you had cancer a while back. How are
you doing?" Before bed, I sent Ira Glass an e-mail saying
that I thought I maybe had a recording that he could use
parts of for an upcoming show, but that I wasn't entirely
sure.

In the morning, I turned my phone on to find all sorts
of different alerts indicating that I had endless e-mails,

texts, and voice mails. There were book offers. *Rolling Stone* magazine was calling and I was trending on Twitter. I couldn't figure out how everyone had found out I had cancer. How had so many people told so many people? I was so touched yet completely dumbfounded. The extent of my social media is posting pictures of my cat to Facebook. I might as well have been wearing a bonnet while being told I was "going viral."

Later that day, Louis C.K. called to tell me that he was convinced I needed to release the recording of the show as an album. He offered to sell it through his website, just as he'd done with his own CDs and specials. I thought he was insane. I couldn't imagine people listening to the show. I thought it wouldn't translate as a recording and was one of those things you had to be there to truly understand. It would be a version of stopping a party in its tracks to tell possibly the world's most boring story for all to hear and be left wondering why your listeners were humoring you. Flattered, I thanked Louis for thinking my show was good enough to transcend that moment in time and hung up perplexed. Perhaps because he was there, he'd seen something more than most would see. I'd always thought a comedy album should be composed of material that you've worked out thoroughly and recorded only after you've roped in your record label, manager, and miscellaneous representation and hired sound engineers on top of the venue's in-house sound engineers. A comedy album didn't just happen because you'd been diagnosed with a deadly disease; wandered onstage; purged untested, vulnerable material while holding back tears; then walked away thinking, "Let's print hundreds of thousands of copies of that. No run-through. One take. It's ready to go."

While I went off to concern myself with doctors, appointments, and surgeries, the interest and the chatter about my show continued to grow. Magazines, newspapers, and radio shows were calling for interviews and writing stories. And when I announced any change in my life or health on my podcast, *Time* magazine reported it as an actual piece of news. My career had gained momentum to a degree that I'd never even considered possible for myself, and it was bittersweet, to say the least. While I was grateful for the support, I couldn't help feeling the whole situation was ironic. This was an opportunity I wanted to experience happy and healthy, not riddled with anxiety about how long I had to live. Each time I was interviewed on a TV show that was recorded and would air at some future date, I pictured the segment ending with a single white sentence telling the viewers that I had passed away and on what date.

People were calling me brave, and saying that I was "battling" cancer, when the fact of the matter was that at any moment I could be found lying on my couch crying or sitting with a blank face while my mind raced through all the possible versions of my future. Whenever I heard my name associated with "bravery," or "battling cancer," I pictured military personnel busting through my front door because they'd heard how brave I was and needed me to replace their buddy who just died on the front lines. They'd see me curled on the couch in a fetal position, wearing my pajamas and crying for my mommy, and say, "Yeah, we need *her*."

My biggest problem with being called brave was that I felt undeserving. I didn't choose to get cancer or to handle it in any particular way. It seemed that what people were calling courageous was simply the fact that I happened to still be breathing. Although I was terrified that the "invasive" part of my diagnosis was unstoppable, I was very aware that there were more dire diagnoses than stage II invasive breast cancer. Yes, trying to be alive with a deadly disease makes a person brave, almost by default. You have to get through a certain number of days dangling in purgatory, unaware if the end of the road is health and happiness or a brutal, painful demise. But what's the alternative—cowardice? Can anyone with a deadly disease be called cowardly? Even those who have lost the will to live?

A month and a half after my Largo show, I finally agreed to release the album. The demands from the press and social media to hear the audio from the show had shown no signs of dying down. People were speculating about what could possibly have been said that was so great that everyone was tweeting and blogging about it. I worried it would be a huge disappointment to everyone and that I'd be mortified. Part of me wanted it to be a show made legendary by word of mouth only, but I finally decided I had to put my ego aside. If my album had the potential to help anyone in a similar predicament, or in any other for that matter, then it was my responsibility as a human being to release it.

My album *Live* was released the day I arrived in New York City to start a new writing job at Comedy Central, which was also the day I was on *Fresh Air* with Terry Gross. I named the album *Live,* as in the verb that means to keep not dying, in part because of the material, but also because I enjoyed the idea of correcting people whenever they pronounced it wrong:

"Oh, I love your album Live."

"Thanks, but it's actually pronounced Live."

Within the first few hours of *Live*'s release, it had sold approximately six thousand copies. Walking down a Manhattan sidewalk with Kyle, who had also moved to New York to work on the show, I got a steady stream of e-mail updates on my phone from Louis. He was eager to send me the climbing sales numbers, and I was certain this was all just an inital burst that would soon dwindle.* I went to bed feeling tremendously relieved and lucky, but also very much like an impostor. It felt like a fluke that I ended up wanting to perform right after I was diagnosed with breast cancer, a fluke that the show went well considering my emotional state and the material, and a fluke that the show went viral and the album sold so many copies.

Before the album came out, I was a relatively successful comedian, but I was not a household name. Within hours after the album came out, I was in the spotlight with incoming offers for press and work on a level I'd never had. Within a month of my album's release, I became the

_____

*. . . which was to become the number-one-selling comedy album around the world for close to six months.

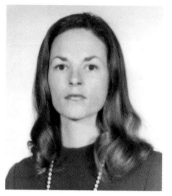

Susie

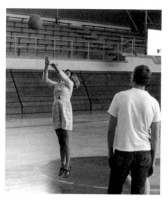

Two points in basketball with the
form of a dancer soon after her coma

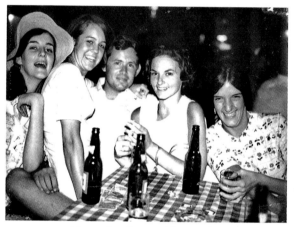

My mother (*second from right*)
with my godmother, Tina (*far left*)

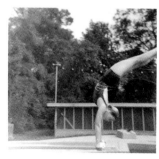

My mother,
the incomparable athlete

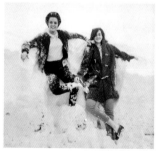

Susie and Tina

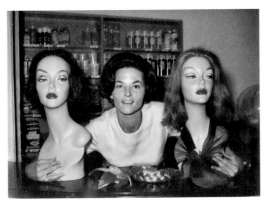

Where's my mother?

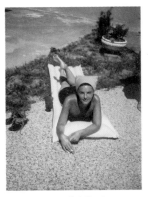

Beautiful Susie

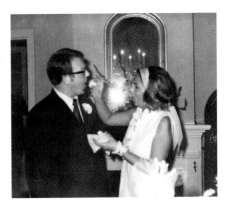

Susie and Pat on their wedding day

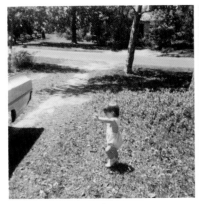

Pat's here!

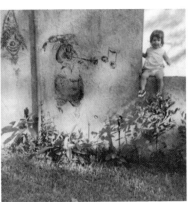

Plopped down next to my
mother's paintings on the back
of our house in Mississippi

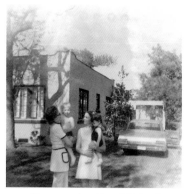

Our grandmother Mildred
visits from Jackson

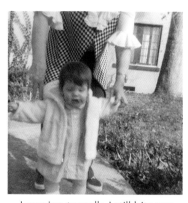

Learning to walk. I still bite my
tongue whenever I concentrate.

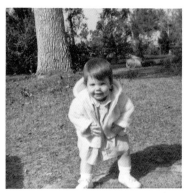

Getting the hang of walking
in my faux fur

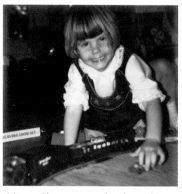

Merry Christmas with a brand new
"Zip" in the background

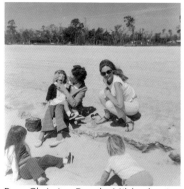

Pass Christian Beach. Mildred trying
to get the sand out of my eyes.

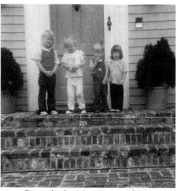

Dirty little Mississippi kids

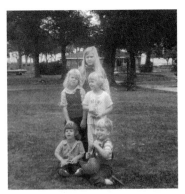

Dirty little Mississippi kids again

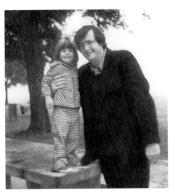

Ric and me

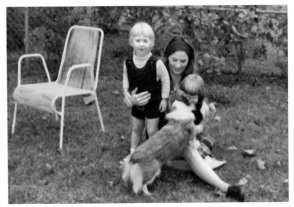

Family photo crashed by neighbor's dog

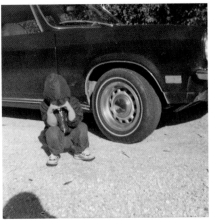

Having a tough day

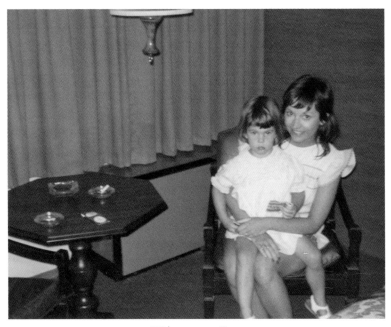

With my aunt Fran

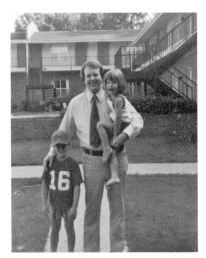
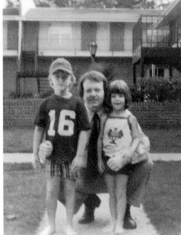

Visiting Pat

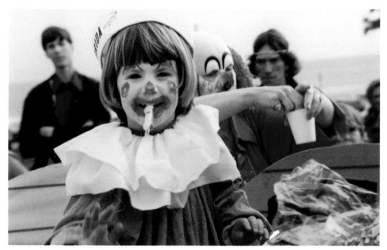

Pass Christian Mardi Gras

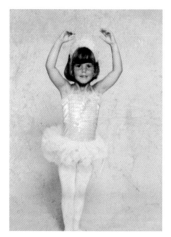

My ballerina glory days

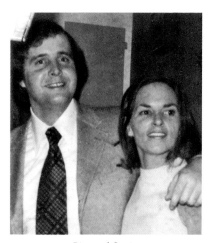

Ric and Susie

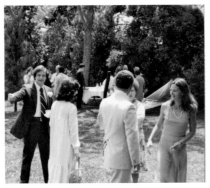

My mother and Ric's wedding
in Pass Christian

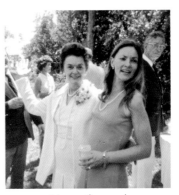

My mother and
my grandmother Teal

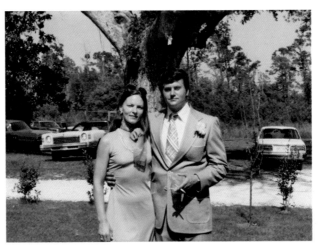

My mother and Uncle Billy

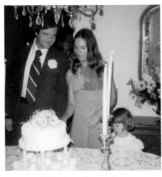

Eyeing the cake

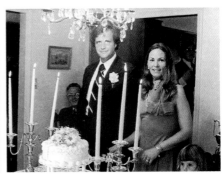

Wedding day

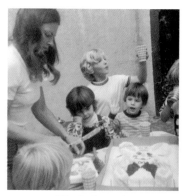

Worth the wait

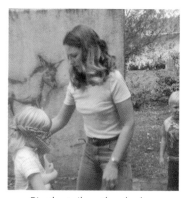

Pin the tail on the donkey
painted on our house

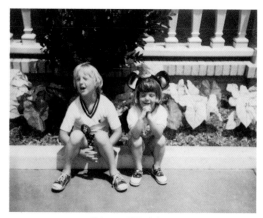

Disney World

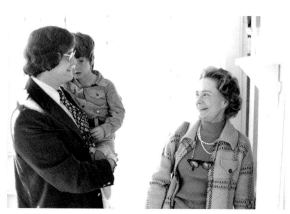

With Ric

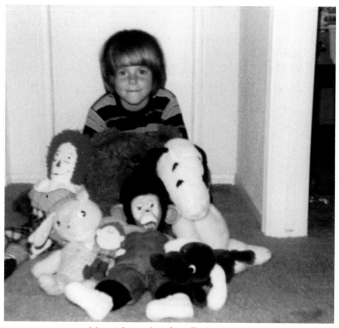

Me with a pile of stuffed animals

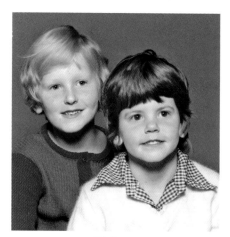

Siblings

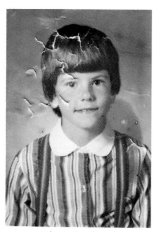

I thought these
patterns matched

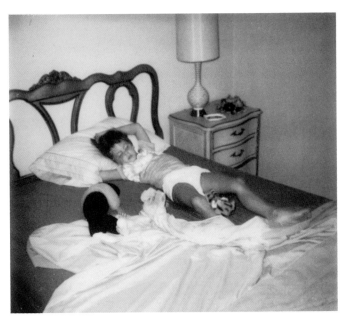

Tomboy nightgown

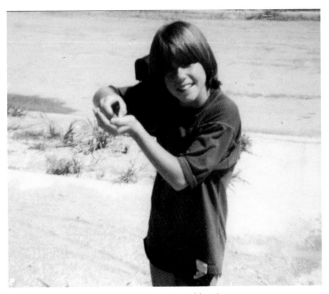

Found an injured bird

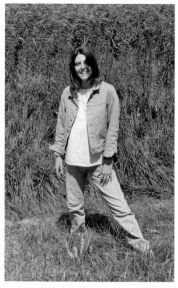

Twenty-one and traveling

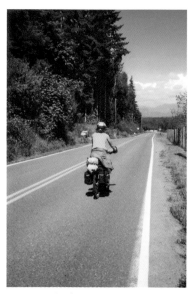

Cycling in Oregon
with my friend Nancy

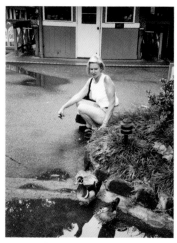

My mother visiting her duck pals

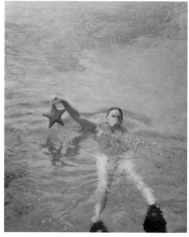

Susie and friend

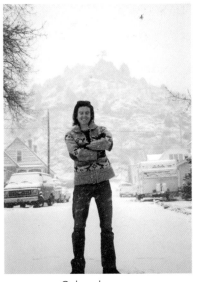

Colorado snow

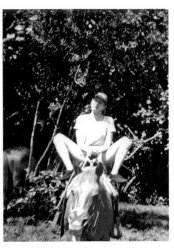

Susie trying to make the
same face as the horse

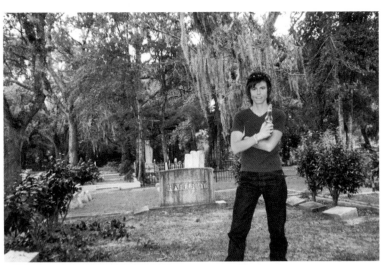

Drinking Barq's in the bottle and visting
Googsie's and Rory's graves in Pass Christian

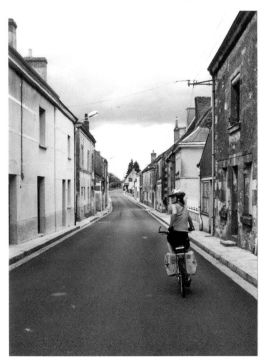

Cycling in France with Shannon

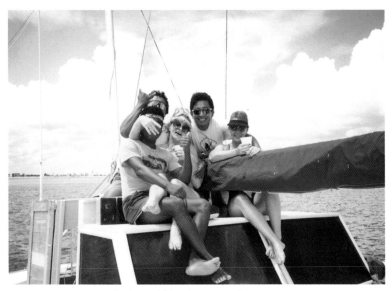

Susie and friends out on the water

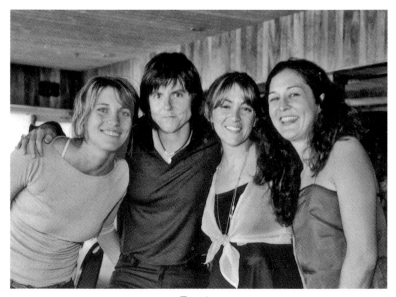

Top tier

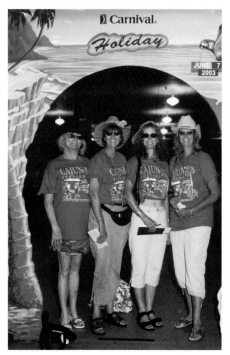

Susie, Sheila, Maxine, and Lisa

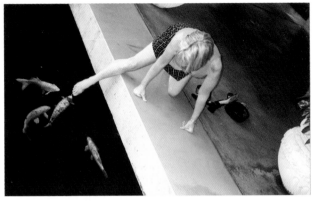

Fish biting my mother's toes

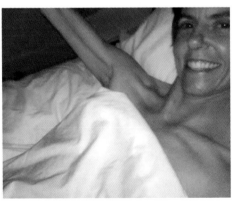

Susie and good friend Cheryl

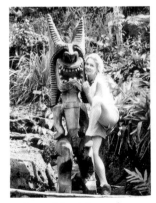

Love this picture of my
mother. Captures her well
toward the end of her life.

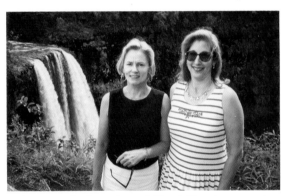

Pneumonia, C-diff, and cancer selfie

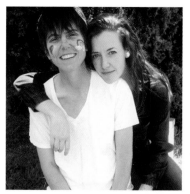

With Stephanie on the set of
my short film *Clown Service*

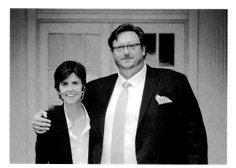

Me and my bro

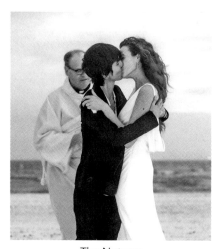

The Notaros

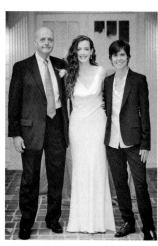

Wedding day with Ric

number-one-selling artist of all time at my record label, Secretly Canadian, which is otherwise composed of only indie rock bands. To this day, Louis tells me that *Live* has sold more copies off his website than his own HBO special did. So I guess what I'm trying to scream at the top of my lungs here is that, basically, my album did all right.

It is very confusing to go from being a comedian at comedy clubs—where half the audience got in for free, not knowing who they were going to see, and the other half recognizes me from another show or late-night appearance—to being a recognizable name who sells out theaters. I always imagined a steady, comfortable climb in my career, even if it was up the world's tiniest steps. I certainly never imagined that success would arrive in tandem with stress, mourning, and deadly disease. I still felt like an impostor.

When I learned that *Live* was being nominated for a Grammy, it was so unreal that I felt detached from the whole ordeal. That much of a spotlight didn't seem like it should be in the cards for me. I almost had to wash my hands of everything because, even though with time I began to understand why the performance had been important, I didn't feel like it was my greatest. The ideas and jokes were not my best. The crowd's response was not the loudest. In truth, I didn't listen to the album with pride. Certain parts still make me cringe. I understand that people enjoyed what felt like eavesdropping on a very raw and candid moment, but if someone had told me as I stood backstage waiting for Ed Helms to wrap up that what I was about to spill out all over that dark room on August 3 would have me nominated for a Grammy, I would have rescheduled so I had time to prepare what I considered possible Grammy Award– winning material.

Ultimately, I didn't end up winning the Grammy, which outraged a lot of people, causing me to frequently hear the phrase "You got robbed!" I certainly don't mind people expressing disappointment that I didn't win, but I don't feel robbed and the phrase "You've been robbed," when it pertains to people who didn't win something or move forward in some contest, makes my skin crawl. It implies that one's belief about somebody's talent is not up for debate. I feel that I am very good at what I do, but I would never think that I am unequivocally the best and deserving of any title. Saying I've been robbed makes me sound like a victim who has had something taken away from her. I never had the Grammy. Nobody moved me forward and then moved me back. Getting nominated, no matter how surreal it seemed, was a move forward that nobody could take away.

People have asked me if it is hard for me that my mother isn't around to see my new level of success, especially when I was being nominated for a Grammy. Well, sure, if my mother knew I'd been nominated for a Grammy she would be squealing at the top of her lungs just like she did when I got my first paid gig and was performing in a smoky saloon with a dusty disco ball over my head. Anytime I called my mother, she reacted as if the world's biggest comedian had picked up the phone in the middle of nowhere and called her. So my answer is no, I don't have a need for my mother to "see me now." I just have the desire to see my mother again.

8

—

Looking Down

The week before my Largo show, when I wasn't sitting around thinking, "I have cancer," I had a distraction besides emptying my bladder from time to time—a gorgeous woman texting me to let me know how adorable she thought I was. I'd met Jessie about five years earlier when we were both acting on the set of *The Sarah Silverman Program*. I'm not religious, but having this particular person pop back into my life, and constantly having her attention, did feel hand-delivered by some greater force.

Our exchanges took me out of my past and my future and made me available to the present, which I could enjoy. These were fleeting moments of happiness in days spent picturing the cancer spreading through my body. My double mastectomy was scheduled for the beginning of September, almost a month after my Largo show, and

I went back and forth between believing I'd come out of surgery and be told I'd be okay and believing I'd be told the cancer had spread to my bones and that I had three years to live—a number I'd arbitrarily decided upon.

This set a limit on the time I could spend with Jessie. I would start to picture us having a fun and crazy fling, or sometimes, more serious partnering where we adopted mix-matched children along the way. I had always wanted to be a mother but had never really pictured how I would get the kids. I knew they probably wouldn't be dropped off by storks, but I also wouldn't have cared if they were. Since my teen years, I had been imagining having a child, and I pictured this only as an image of me riding a bicycle with some sort of blob of a baby in the basket between the handlebars. I saw the blob and me as the best of friends, caring for each other and needing each other. Part of my connection with Jessie was her desire to have children as well. After several unsuccessful pregnancies, she was actively researching adoption possibilities. Even though I had never been able to conceive of committing to a lifelong partner, and especially could not now, I allowed myself the freedom and joy of sitting on the couch with her, browsing adoption websites and scrolling through the precious little faces that were just as in need as we were. I began to picture ten of these little faces in my basket between my handlebars, and then I would remember the harsh reality: "Oh yeah, my body's killing itself." Sometimes it felt like I'd won the lottery on the very day my head was locked in a guillotine. I'd met a beautiful woman who also wanted children, and we were planning our futures separately, but side by side, without pressuring each other for a committed relationship, and yet there was still little opportunity to freely relish the moment. Turn your head to look at what is good in life and maybe get a "Wheeeee!" out before the blade drops and your head rolls down a hill and into a peasant's boot.

Three weeks before my surgery, Jessie invited me to fly up and spend the weekend with her in Toronto, where she was filming a TV show. She assured me we'd have a blast, but it felt so reckless to get a cancer diagnosis and then toss my flip-flops into a bag and head off to another country for a romantic summer escapade. If you have cancer, don't you need to be home freaking out about having cancer? I called my friend Jason, one of my regular go-tos for girl talk, and he immediately interrupted my account of my dilemma with "You have cancer. Go to Toronto. Why are we even having this conversation?"

The next morning I flew to Toronto, thinking, "What

the hell am I doing flying to Toronto?" But in retrospect, this was my Make-a-Wish Weekend. Not only did Jessie frequently serenade me on her guitar, but by the time we rented the fastest speedboat we could find, we'd already gone to Niagara Falls, ordered room service, and explored the entire city of Toronto by foot. We cruised around Lake Ontario blasting a local eighties station, and well, well, well, if "One Night Love Affair" by Bryan Adams wasn't the first song we heard. When a giant cruise ship came near, I steered us in circles around it, and we burst into hysterical laughter when we realized the song we were now blaring as we chopped the waves at the highest speed possible was The Police's mellow and harmonious "Every Breath You Take."

As we flew across the water, it occurred to me that I had the ultimate excuse to get out of anything: "I have cancer." How do you argue with that? But having the biggest excuse was actually no excuse. It seemed like all the more reason to make an effort to connect with someone. "I'm busy," "I'm tired," "I have to work" now seemed really lame. While you're alive, you should feel alive. I thought about how tomorrow or a week from now, or whatever date people tell themselves is the big day—a party, an award show, a holiday—is no more important than the event of today. I thought: "Every day *is the day*."

On September 4, I went in for surgery. My aunt Fran, my father Pat's sister who I am close to, had driven up from Oceanside to spend the night before surgery with me and then take me to the hospital. Sarah and Mark Flanagan met me in the lobby at 6 A.M. The first thing Sarah did when she saw me was look at my chest and say, "Oh my God—am I too late? Did you already have it done?" It was a nice break in the tension everyone felt. We all chatted while I checked in, and kept it casual, but everyone was aware that something major was about to happen. I was mostly able to pretend it wasn't major until I was in a gown and lying on a gurney. Everything seemed muffled as I was being wheeled down the hall. I had debated whether or not to take a picture of myself before the surgery, but I rarely looked through any old photos in the first place. When would I get out the shoe box of my old vacation photos and topless selfies sporting boobs riddled with cancer? I had decided I needed to embrace my new reality and keep moving forward, and now here I was, moving forward. I was in a kind of capsule, hearing the murmur of people talking, the wheels rolling. In my mind, a big metal bar was locking down in front of me as

I dragged my fingernails along the walls of the hospital, trying to hold on. I was at the top of the world's steepest roller coaster, and I could almost hear the *click, click, click* of what I really hoped wouldn't be a one-way ride.

Then I woke up. I lived. Maybe everything would be okay? Because my blood pressure had dropped very low during surgery, the doctors had to wait on giving me more anesthesia, so I was very aware that I had a new body. "Hmm," I thought, "this must be exactly what it feels like to have a double mastectomy." I was in a fog of Dilaudid once again when my surgeon came in. She was kind and had a great bedside manner. It seemed entirely impossible that this friendly, easygoing woman had just finished cutting into my flesh and pulling out globs of tissue. She smiled and said she had some good news: She believed the cancer had not spread and that she had gotten it all. *A-L-L.* My drug-induced state made it hard for me to understand just how good this news was or to even realize what else I thought or felt other than the sensation of looking up.

A nonstop stream of friends came by, but I was so jacked up on painkillers that my hospital room looked like a party going on around someone who had overdosed before the guests had arrived. My face was greasy, my tits were off, and it looked like a horse had been chewing on my hair since 1977. The only thing I had going for me at this point was that I could (barely) use the bathroom on my own.

The day I was discharged from the hospital after my double mastectomy, I was ordered to take it easy, which made sense because I was sewn up, bandaged, and in a lot of pain, but instead I went to the Stand Up to Cancer benefit TV taping that I had been invited to as a special guest of the producers. I didn't want to be halfway between not better and better. I wanted to go from cancer back to my normal life without missing a beat. Watching everyone socialize at the after-party made me feel normal for a moment. No one knew that a couple of hours before, I'd been at the hospital, chest-deep in cancer. But soon I began to feel separate from everyone, like I was in a fishbowl, or too young to play with the big kids. Waves of light-headedness, weakness, and nausea came over me, and standing up became nearly impossible. I didn't want to be standing up to cancer; I wanted to go lie down with it.

This was the beginning of me being home all the time in bed and relying on people in ways that I had to become comfortable with really fast. For a month, I would be at the mercy of kind friends who fought for the chance to bring me food, help me get dressed, and drain the blood and gunk coming from my chest—my chest, which I couldn't bring myself to look at. My fear of looking down was compounded by the fact that I'm someone who is extremely queasy—almost phobic—when it comes to any sort of fresh injury to the human body, or to any creature, for that matter. I often imagine how unhelpful I'd be running up to the wreckage of a car crash hoping to help but promptly vomiting and fainting at the sight of blood. I'd be mistakenly life-flighted to the nearest hospital while the real victim waited for AAA to haul their mangled body to a junkyard. I discovered my almost phobic aversion to blood and guts in seventh grade when we were asked to dissect an earthworm. I couldn't believe the ease with which my eager classmates heartlessly eviscerated their specimens with pins and razors. Ironically, almost a decade later, my first job in Hollywood would be working for Sam Raimi (name drop), the master director of horror and blood splatter.

Despite being unable to deal with looking down, I did have to face my chest's future. I had met with several reconstructive surgeons, and each meeting left me wondering why on earth I would ever go through such intense procedures just to have fake boobs. My chest was barely anything at all to begin with, so why go through such pain and recovery time for something that wouldn't be noticed? It's not like I'd be opting to get porn jugs on my second go-round. I'd essentially be surgically attaching the equivalent of two kiwis, less hair, no stickers. I tried to picture taking my shirt off in front of someone with these fake things attached to me and saying, "Welp, here's my boobs!" But I could never imagine being truly comfortable with that situation; it always felt like a punch line. So, I settled on no reconstructive surgery, which meant no boobs, no nipples, just nice, uneven scars.

It took the prospect of surgery for me to realize how much I had actually loved my body. I didn't want it to be different. And after surgery, I felt so damaged. The place where I had once considered myself "flat-chested" was now slightly concave and padded with thick bandages, throbbing with a dull ache and with frequent sharp, shooting pains. Pulling T-shirts on and off was nearly impossible, and I was mostly confined to button-down shirts. I felt too vulnerable to exist outside of my apartment. The thought of walking down the street stirred fears of being punched in the chest; the thought of getting into a car was accompanied by the sight of the ensuing accident where my chest hit the steering wheel and was ripped wide open. Again.

When the doctor removed my bandages, my chest was almost teasing me to look down. Instead, I Googled images of "bilateral double mastectomy." The worse the photos looked, the more certain I was that my chest looked like that. Taking a sponge bath meant moving a washcloth over my chest, trying to clean very bruised and battered flesh without forming a mental image of what was beneath the cloth. I never let myself glance down. Even when I was able to start showering, I let the running water clean my chest while I stared straight at the ceiling.

One morning when I was brushing my teeth, I leaned toward my mirror and caught a startling glimpse of swollen, bruised flesh crisscrossed with black stitching, which made me feel as though I had indeed been in a horrible accident instead of expertly tended to by a surgeon. From that morning on, I buttoned my shirt up to the very top when I brushed my teeth. That grisly sight confirmed that I didn't want to see any more of what I was now calling my "Frankenchest." But someone had to. And unfortunately for her, it was my friend Lake. She had come over for a visit, and after chatting for several hours on my couch while sipping room-temperature tap water, I asked if she'd look at my chest—a typical move on my part, I must say. She agreed, but I could sense her fear as I slowly lifted my shirt. Immediately I saw relief in her face. "Tiggy," she said. "You can do this. You can totally do this."

A couple of days later, I stood in front of a mirror and slowly unbuttoned my shirt. When I looked down, what I saw turned out to be just a flat chest with fresh scars on their way to looking healed. My stitches had dissolved. I took my shirt completely off and stared at myself, thinking, "Lake was right, I can do this." I could totally do this.

A month later, I moved to New York City to write and appear on Comedy Central's new show *Inside Amy Schumer*. I shared a bedroom in Chelsea with Kyle, and although I felt light-years beyond where I had been even a month earlier, I also felt wobbly and unstable. I was joining a writer's room that had started several weeks before. My body was different, my family was different, and my sense of self felt less reliable. Always looming heavily in my mind was the fact that both the diseases that could have killed me might return at any time. Every choice I made—what to eat, where to go, who to be around—was tied directly to my health and what I had been through. Looking back, I had probably come out of the woods a little too recently to already be stepping onto an over-crowded subway car and rattling through Manhattan with no nipples.

I couldn't fully hug people yet, but I could walk down the street feeling cautious rather than fearful. I had looked down while showering many times in the past month, but with great mental preparation. Soon after arriving in New York, I showered and found myself mindlessly looking down at my chest and was shocked that I was shocked to see nothing. This meant that for a few moments it had completely slipped my mind that I'd even had surgery or that cancer had been inside my body.

My surprise in the shower meant I was making seri-ous progress with my recovery and self-image, but I was still not completely back to being myself. Every evening, Kyle did stand-up sets around town, and though I would normally be doing it with him, I wasn't on my game. I was often clouded and lost in thought. What had just hap-pened to my life?! I felt suspended in time, like this wasn't my reality. "How did I get here?" This was a question I still didn't know the answer to even though I knew ex-actly how I got here: I was a stand-up comic who got cancer and was now working as a television writer in New York City. Feeling suspended in time was not necessarily bad. Kyle and I had been bursting into hysterics at the idea of getting bunk beds and having a combined age of eighty-three, and then one day we went out and bought bunk beds. It was a nearly surreal happiness to lie on the top bunk in the dark every night with Kyle on the bottom bunk, both of us laughing to no end. I felt like I was existing in some happy moment of my childhood, laughing in a bunk bed with my best friend while peering down at my chest, flat as an eight-year-old's, in a T-shirt.

Mostly, I spent my time in New York trying to enjoy a much-needed invisibility. The problem was that I also knew a ton of people in the City, and I had a huge story to tell, so nothing was a quick catch-up. The press wouldn't stop either. *Rolling Stone,* the *New York Times, Fresh Air* with Terry Gross, *Time* magazine, interviews, photo shoots, hair/makeup appointments. I don't mean to sound like I'm complaining or bragging—I certainly appreciated the new job, the new city, the new diagnosis of good health, and the new press, to a degree—but it was very complicated to be emerging from that dark and seemingly never-ending tunnel and facing a tsunami of attention and expectation.

Jessie also happened to be temporarily living in New York City while she starred in an off-Broadway musical. One night, she invited me over while she was cat-sitting for her friend Gina, who had a ridiculously beautiful apartment overlooking some river. I got into bed wearing my T-shirt. It was winter and the heater was cranked. The apartment was outrageously hot. I told Jessie that I was sorry, but I needed to take off my shirt. She said, "Of course," and lay back to wait.

I was now facing the exact moment I had been dreading. Lake had seen my Frankenchest, but she was a friend. This was my first topless romantic encounter. I wasn't sure it would go well even though Jessie had previously given me the impression that not only was this no big deal, it was something that she was *way* into.

We had been out to dinner a few weeks after my surgery, when I was still struggling to look down, and I asked if it would freak her out to see my scars. She said that it wouldn't. I asked again, and she replied that no, it wouldn't freak her out at all. I asked her one more time just to make sure and she said, "To be totally honest, I fucking love scars!" Wow. This had been the last possible thing I'd expected to hear. She loves scars?! That's too good to be true. She loves scars?! Oh my gosh—Jessie,

I can hook you up, no problem. If there's one thing I do have to bring to this relationship, by God, it's scars. The amount of confidence she gave me that night at the restaurant is beyond words. I went from uncomfortably adjusting and readjusting my shirts to hide my new body to wanting to wear fitted T-shirts, and it was all because Jessie said she thought scars were sexy.

Now, in Gina's bed, was the moment of truth. Jessie was about to either find things really sexy or find out how much she didn't actually fucking love scars. I sat up on my knees facing her as she was lying down and took off my T-shirt to reveal my bare chest with its two-inch scars in place of my two-inch breasts. "Oh my God! You're so hot!" she said, pulling me toward her. "You look so fucking sexy!" she exclaimed. Wait a minute, she's talking to me, right? Indeed she was.

Someone looking at you just the way you are and exclaiming that you're hot always feels great, but when you look a way that you never thought you would look, you really want to hear someone say it's so fucking hot.

A few weeks later, I got to test that confidence while shooting an episode of Amy's show. Although the episode ended up airing after several other TV appearances I made on other shows, it was the first time I had taped something for national television since my surgery. I was wearing a fitted baseball jersey, and my posture was not confident. The scene required several takes, and in between them, I snuck off to peer at my reflection in the surrounding windows to see if my scars were clearly visible. It appeared that they were not, but I shot the entire episode worried that my scars would be making their national television debut through the powerful lens of the camera. I kept wanting to stop the production and ask, "Hey, can you guys see my scars?" Instead, I said my lines while slouched with my hands shoved in my pockets, picturing my scars moving from extras in the background to scars of the show.

When I returned home from New York, I looked anxiously around my apartment. I had not been there for any substantial amount of time since everything had turned inside out, and coming home to the stillness of my life before it all changed was almost haunting. My unmade bed, my last few outfits in the hamper, my dirty cup in the sink, the magazine issue dated from the month that I last steadily occupied this apartment. It was the scene before the crime. The picture before the crash. I was staring at my naivete, my assumption that life would continue to go on right where it had left off.

I spent an entire day in and out of a paralyzing panic attack. I could only sit very still on my couch, trying to breathe. The ground beneath my feet seemed to have become a tightrope, and sitting on my couch didn't feel safe; it felt like I was about to lose my balance and fall off not only the couch, but the planet entirely. I spent hours sitting still, trying to picture myself as a solid, stationary body. I felt that same quiet and quick unraveling that sometimes overcomes me on airplanes when I'm strapped in my seat, wondering what it would look like if I actually let go just a little and let my fear and anxiety have their way. Would I open the exit door to jump and let everyone get sucked out with me? Sitting in my apartment, I needed to scream and run and jump somewhere. The wide-open space of my downtown loft welcomed that kind of wildly uncool display of angst, but I just physically couldn't do it.

I guess being anonymous and misplaced in New York had stalled the final attack of fear and anxiety about all that had happened to me, because a few days later, on the morning of January 1, 2013, I landed right back into my body, feeling like the world's most experienced and knowledgeable infant. Everything felt sorted and compartmentalized in a way that my psyche could process.

I felt reborn. Breathing was as easy as doing nothing. I was light and available to life again. I no longer felt heavy under the pressure to perform comedy and was eager to put myself out in front of audiences and answer the question of what I was going to say next and how, if at all, my stand-up would change.

Open and ready to embark on a new life, I toddled out of my grown-up apartment into the brightness of life to do errands. I lived in the hippest part of downtown L.A., full of cafés, juice bars, and top Zagat-rated restaurants, and if I strolled just one block east, I was sure to be murdered. I headed west, toward my Volkswagen. Had I been wearing a hat that day, I would have tossed it in the air like Mary Tyler Moore.

"You're gonna make it after all . . ."

9

God Never Gives You More Than You Can Handle

I once saw a video of someone crossing themselves as they jumped from one of the Twin Towers before it collapsed. And I was certain that, if there was a "God," they must, occasionally, give people more than they can handle.

I had heard the phrase "God never gives you more than you can handle" my whole life and I believed it in the same way I believed that when one door closes, another one opens. But both of these truisms come up short. What if you don't have a door, or what if you do, but your door never fully opens?

Also, prayer can be narcissistic. If a mother believes that God has answered her prayers because her child's soccer team won the game, she must also believe that God ignored the other team's prayers. Just like that particular God must have ignored the prayers of those who were being beaten and raped. But hey, maybe those individuals could just handle more. On the off chance that there *is* a God who can hear prayers, but can't hear all of them at once, then the people who are praying for goals to be scored, good seats, and sunshine are clogging up the prayer line.

It's like the song "Do They Know It's Christmas?," which describes how lucky we are to not be in Africa, "Where the only water flowing is the bitter sting of tears / And the Christmas bells that ring there / Are the clanging chimes of doom," and tells the listener to "thank God it's them, instead of you." I mean, what on earth? Even when I was a child, this stuck out to me. I loved the tune and the catchiness of the lyrics, but when I really concentrated on what I was singing, I thought about how that prayer might go: "God, thank you so much for making other people starve to death and not me."

During my wretched four months, I heard "God never gives you more than you can handle" way more than I could handle. But I can assure you that C-diff, the death of my mother, and breast cancer were each, individually, more than I could handle. For all of them to essentially be happening at the same time—peppered with a breakup—put me way beyond my limit. I mean, it really felt like enough when I had pneumonia. If that had been all that happened to me in 2012, then I would be saying, "Holy cow, I had *pneumonia* in 2012."

As soon as my cancer was in remission, I started hearing, "God is good," perhaps as a knee-jerk response to good news, or because it was certain well-meaning people's response to God answering their prayers that I would be okay. If the cancer had spread and was going to kill me, I highly doubt that the news would have elicited a "God is good." Instead, I would die and the same people would say, "God called her home." Does God have a great big plan that we are all watching unfold? If that's the case, why did my mother have to get clubbed in the head while she was being called home? I guess this is one of those times when God works in mysterious ways?

Sometimes, when I heard, "God is good," I imagined two patients lying next to each other in a cancer center. One of them is being told that they are in remission and their visitor announces that God has answered their prayers. What if the nearby terminal patient interrupted to ask them, "What about me and my prayers?" Would anyone really look at someone who is dying and in physical pain and say, "I guess your prayers went unanswered, but just remember, sometimes unanswered prayers are a gift"?

My biggest problem with people who talk about God and prayers is how confident they are about how it all works out until it doesn't work out. This kind of willful blindness astounds me. If something is a miracle when it works, then when it doesn't work that should not just be ignored; it should be questioned. The opposite of a miracle is not nothing. It's totally not a miracle.

If I were dying and someone who believes in a God who can hear prayers turned to me and said, "Unfortunately, Tig, God didn't hear your prayers, and this is a gift," I would be thrilled. I might be dying, but at least I would have lived long enough to finally get the chance to witness a person bold enough to not waver in what they claim to believe simply because it's convenient to do so.

Since I received my official certificate marking me as an expert of "What to Say to Someone Enduring Sadness and Despair"—which I can assure you is hung next to my framed and adorably nibbled GED that nobody, except literally my cat, has ever given a shit about—I feel qualified to tell you that it's important to assess what that distressed person's needs may be. Is this a person who wants to hear about God and religion right now? Or ever? Or is this someone who only wants a sounding board? Having to comfort someone with a deadly disease is in no way a highly sought-after position and most people are probably doing the best they can. I am certain they were for me. But what I needed to hear most was something that was connected to the moment—to undeniable reality. When I heard, "Wow, that sounds really hard," or even an awkward "I don't know what to say . . ." it was tremendously comforting. I felt as though someone was really talking to me and considering what was actually going on, and, most importantly, was willing to succumb to the moment instead of covering it up with a one-size-fits-all platitude. I imagine that most people in my situation, regardless of their religious beliefs, would want the opportunity to express the depths of their fears, concerns, and questions without being showered with blind and deaf positivity.

When I was afraid I might die, my emotions needed out, they didn't need to be squelched with false assurance.

In case there really is a God, and He-She-It didn't judge this book by its cover and is reading this, let me be very clear: Losing my ability to eat food—and more than twenty pounds—as well as losing my mother; losing my breasts; having stitched and scabbed incisions across my chest that made it almost impossible to be hugged or to move; being unable to lift my arms until I was able to re-build excised muscle tissue; being terrified of dying, and if I lived, of never working again; and going through a breakup while having constant stabbing pains in my gut was, ultimately, more than I could handle.

10

R2, Where Are You?

From time to time when I was little, I was referred to as Li'l Pig-Pen. Every toy and stuffed animal I owned had to be easily reachable from the floor or kept under the antique bed, which was a couple of feet off the floor—one of my favorite places to play. The hallway was also teeming with stuffed animals since it was the waiting area for customers hoping to be seated at the very popular restaurant I co-owned with my stuffed monkey, Zip. We served plastic hot dogs and hamburgers and bottomless teacups full of Listerine to every giraffe, dolphin, and Raggedy Ann and Andy under our roof.

When it came time for cleanup, my stepfather, Ric, took charge. There was no messing around with Ric. His military-style punishments were as intimidating as his substantial size. I was given an allotted time to clean my

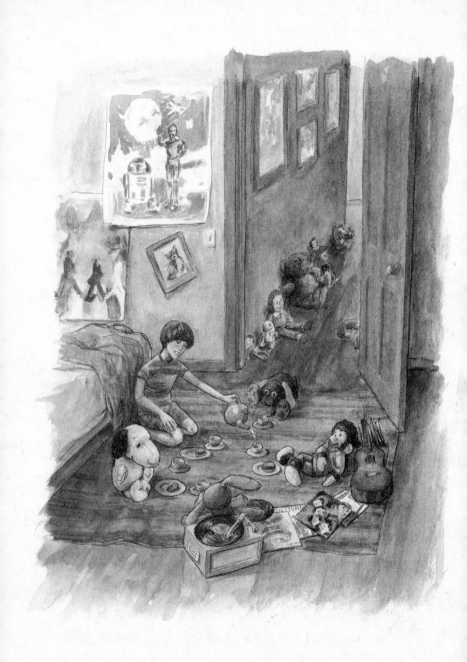

room, and I would hear his warnings coming from the couch, where he usually sat, sipping scotch and watching the nightly news: "You have thirty more minutes!"; "You have fifteen more minutes!"; "Better hurry it up, Tig!"

To me, cleaning my room meant shoving plastic horses, baseball bats, a cowboy boot, and my business partner, Zip, under my bed or behind the dresser.

To Ric—who was a very thorough person—cleaning meant organizing drawers, or even better, throwing things in the trash. When my time was up, he'd walk into my room with an empty trash bag to inspect my cleanup job. I begged and pleaded as he looked under my bed, behind my dresser, and every other place some little thing's face was sticking out of, and without hesitation or discussion shoved everything into the sack and immediately locked it in the trunk of his car. His attitude was one of "too bad." It was like the opposite of Christmas, Santa in reverse. The only "ho ho ho" was the sound of me whimpering through my tears as I was informed that I'd have to do some chores to earn money to buy my toys back. It was pretty intense, but to be fair, they were all for sale at a much discounted rate. The Millennium Falcon would go for around a nickel at most.

Growing up, I joked that Ric was like C-3PO, but

with less emotion. As the years passed, it dawned on me that the joke never really made any sense, because C-3PO was actually quite emotional, throwing his shiny metal arms around, yelling, "R2! R2! We're doomed!! Where are you, R2?!"

Ric was just robotic. He didn't even cry when he cut onions, which, despite having been a cook in the army and a gourmet chef, he very rarely did. Perhaps once a year, he'd make a delicious four-course meal. It wasn't a festive occurrence; it was him in the kitchen with all his appliances at the ready, cooking and meticulously cleaning as he went. As I write this, I don't even know what lit the spark in him to get up to cook. Seeing Ric get up and do anything that wasn't going to work, watching TV, eating dinner, or going to bed was perplexing, an anomaly that unleashed a covert excitement in our family: *Oh, look, Ric's mowing the lawn. Look at that! Ric's answering the telephone.*

I have memories as a child of getting very excited when Ric got into the pool with us and tossed us around in the water. Which means that at age five, I already knew an interaction with Ric was something not to take for granted. As I got older, I told myself that it probably just wasn't in Ric's nature to want to be around other humans or to expend his energy on anything more than his work, though he seemed to always have an unreasonable amount of energy available for giving the carton of orange juice a good shake. And I mean a good shake. Every inch of him was thrown into the action—to the point where my mother, Renaud, and I would be laughing from the shock of seeing his body move so quickly and freely.

"Well, too bad," was the typical response Ric gave to anyone in his immediate family when they shared their concerns or frustrations. If I had a problem with someone in school, Ric's advice was "Well, don't talk to him anymore." If I had a problem with a loud neighbor as an adult, telling Ric about it went like this:

"My neighbor is so noisy."

"Well, then find a new apartment."

"But, I can't. I'm on a lease and—"

"Well, you should move out."

"But—"

"If you don't move out, I have no sympathy for you."

Throughout my childhood, Ric provided financial support and material things, stability and security. He tossed in a home-cooked meal here or there and kind but very emotionally controlled "I love you's," but I never got the feeling he knew how to be there at my side as I figured things out in life. For certain, he wasn't someone to bounce things off of. His thinking felt very black-and-white. When I told Ric anything that I was concerned about or that happened to me, he usually implied that it was either trivial or my fault. Even with my mother's emotional support and very passionate displays of affection, I was always left needing more from Ric.

The day that "parents" popped up on my cell phone in March of 2012, no part of me thought to expect anything other than my mother's cheery, loving voice. When Ric's hollowed, devastated voice barely made it through the receiver, leaving me the message that my mother had had a tragic fall and was not going to make it, part of me understood that "parents," from this point on, was going to mean something very different. Sometime later that day, it hit me hard: "Oh my gosh, this man that my mother met and brought into our lives and ultimately married is now 'parents.'"

On my journey home to take my mother off life support, I thought about Ric on his wedding day about to marry my mother at my aunt and uncle's house in Pass Christian. I imagined him somehow acquiring the knowledge that my mother would have a tragic fall in 2012, and I pictured him watching my four-year-old self playing in the yard and thinking about how, in thirty-seven years, he would have to tell this little girl in front of him that her mother wasn't going to make it. He would have thirty-seven years to get ready to make that phone call. But could he? No one could. It was clear that as each word came out of his mouth, it stunned him. There had always been an assumption in our family, which was acknowledged after the death of my mother, that Ric would be the first to go.

In many ways, Ric being my parent only made sense with my mother still alive. With her gone, I wasn't sure I would ever hear from him again. What were we going to offer each other? I no longer needed material things or financial support. I no longer would call the house and talk with him briefly before asking for my mother. So what now?

After my mother's death, I wanted to have an openness toward Ric. I knew he could cry. He cried in the hospital and at my mother's funeral. Then there was the drive home from her funeral, which made me eager to feel and create a sense of family with him.

It was a seven-hour drive from my mother's funeral in Pass Christian back to Spring, Texas, and I drove with Ric. The only other time I had driven from Mississippi to Texas with him was when I was four years old. He and my mother had just married and Ric was driving his new family of one wife, two cats, two kids, and several nearly dead potted plants that my mother insisted we move to our new house. The journey took three days because of all the bathroom stops, backseat fights, and meows. Just to emphasize, it was a seven-hour drive and it took us three days. The first day, we tackled driving over the bridge into the neighboring town of Bay St. Louis and checked into a hotel for the night. I can't imagine that we logged much more than four miles total.

Being alone in the car with Ric for seven hours after my mother's funeral was awkward. We'd been crying side by side for the past five days, but it sometimes seemed like an isolated grief. Ric's emotions were new to me and, to some degree, being strapped in the car with him just an arm's length away was like being forced to experience my mother's death with someone I was meeting for the first time. To be fair, neither of us is a tremendously affectionate person. Now we had seven hours and nothing and everything to talk about.

I drove, and Ric and I began chatting about politics and religion, our typical topics of conversation. After a couple of hours of this, he told me he'd like to discuss a conversation we'd had a few years back. At first, I had no idea what he was referring to. Finally he said, "It was the conversation where you said I hurt your feelings when I told you I thought you should quit comedy to go to business school." I immediately remembered the hurtful conversation. He had said my career was a waste of my intelligence and my time, that I should look into business school or something along those lines. I had said, "So, if I told you I was going to leave my life and career that has brought me so much happiness and success to go work at a job I had no interest in, in a cubicle somewhere, and have the life sucked out of me, you'd support that?!" He said, "Yes, absolutely." More than hurt, I had been shocked by his words because I had made up in my head that Ric was proud of me and had accepted the fact that I hadn't taken the typical route in life but had succeeded anyway.

I told him I remembered the conversation and

watched in astonishment as his lip began to quiver. Soon he was crying and saying he was sorry he ever said any of that. As horrible as it may sound, it felt good to see him cry so hard he couldn't talk. When he was able to speak, he admitted that he had projected his ideas of how life should go based on the route he had taken himself. He said he never related to me or understood me because of this. He declared that he now realized it's not the child's responsibility to teach the parent who they are; it's the parent's responsibility to learn who their child is.

I felt like I was watching hell freeze over. This day was never supposed to happen. I didn't realize how much I had needed Ric to give me the freedom to be me—and, consequently, to give himself enough freedom to admit he had been wrong. Although I would have given anything to have some other reason for the drive we were making, even if it was just to move nearly dead potted plants across three states, Ric's display of emotion was a sign of life I needed to see. My mother was dead and my stepfather, who had always seemed so dead inside, had come alive. The robot was changing.

For the next hour, Ric went on to admit that he'd worked too much when I was young and didn't spend enough time getting to know me or my brother. He said he was proud of me and thought that I should no doubt be doing comedy because he believed it was my gift. He marveled over me not going to any sort of school to learn my craft and said that he couldn't believe how well I'd done without anyone's help. Tears were rolling down my face the entire time he spoke. I quietly listened and drove us home, thinking how amazing this was but also how sad since my mother was not able to see it happen.

Of course, the conversation Ric and I were having probably wouldn't have happened if my mother had been alive and sitting in the backseat of the car. Ric and I both seem to hold back our true feelings until it's safe to release them. I know for certain that having my mother begin to disappear with dementia and then into death cleared the way for me to express my true feelings. My mother wasn't there to misinterpret my apologies as me finally coming around and taking full blame for all of our struggles. She couldn't burst with excitement at the first hint of my vulnerability and scare me away from revealing more. I wish my feelings hadn't needed this kind of blank slate. I wish my mother had never become a blank slate. But they did, and she did. Why is this so often true of human relationships? Why can so many of us only express our true feelings onto a blank slate: a diary page, the sky, an unconscious loved one, a tombstone?

In the car, I thanked Ric for telling me what was clearly so hard for him to say, and let him know that it wasn't too little too late. My mother's death had made me realize how important it is to not write people off so easily. Instead of being someone who expects people to have all the strengths I think I need them to have, I resolved to try to become someone who focuses on the strengths they do have. And to believe people can change. I thought this was going to be a challenge, and boy, was I right.

For Thanksgiving, Ric and Renaud and I went to Austin to celebrate with Ric's side of the family. I was welcomed by everyone, but I didn't know most of the people, which only made it more obvious that my mother was missing. The following day, I needed time alone and decided to drive to Houston and spend a night at my mother and Ric's house to clear my head. My feelings were at bay for most of the drive until I reached the Houston city limits and felt a heavy ache in my chest. Seven months earlier, I had spent over a month in my mother's home without her and had been to her funeral, but pulling up to the house felt eerily like approaching a crime scene. Everything seemed too quiet and scary. I sat in the driveway, crying. When I was able to find the nerve to enter the house, I walked around slowly taking in the smell and looking at the scattered photos left where my mother had placed them over the years. Each picture seemed not only to capture a moment but really to freeze time. I felt as though I had walked into an abandoned house with pictures of a family that had long since disappeared. All their moments had long since disappeared. I picked up each photo and stared at our faces, thinking, "I wonder what your story is."

I began opening drawers looking for little notes my mother would have written herself as reminders. I searched for her wallet, or anything, really, that could tangibly connect me to her. But each drawer and closet I opened was emptier than the last. Everything was gone. Things need to have a purpose or a use for Ric to keep them, and I knew he would gut the house, but I didn't think he would do it so soon. I had to fight to keep my monkey, Zip, in the storage closet, where he had been enjoying his retirement for more than thirty years after the closure of our restaurant because Ric claimed that Zip, along with everything else from my childhood, was a fire hazard and should be removed from the house or thrown away. Ric and my mother regularly argued over the storage of things precious to her that he wanted to toss out.

I ran from room to room looking for anything of my mother's, angry that I had fallen for Ric's vulnerability on our car ride home. I was furious that Ric didn't see how my mother's things would have a purpose for me. He hadn't changed at all. I was certain I was done with him. *This* was who Ric was, and I was realizing I couldn't be the person I was hoping to be. I was ready to cut him out of my life. I called him, full of rage, and accused him of throwing out all of my mother's stuff. How dare he! How could he! What was he thinking! He interrupted and asked me to wait one second, that things were not how they appeared. Very openly and kindly he guided me over the phone back to his and my mother's bedroom closet and described where he had safely stored a few of my mother's belongings for me to keep. On the top shelf there was another pair of her ballet slippers, a sweater, a box of her jewelry, a blanket, and one of her paintings. I was relieved and touched. If not a little shocked. Ric was trying. He seemed to have some emotional understanding of where I was coming from, which was something completely new in our relationship. Did he naturally do this? Or did the robot reprogram himself to do it? Ideally, Ric would have left all of my mother's things for me to continue to find and keep as I opened drawers, even her notes to herself and sketches on napkins. But he didn't. This was Ric's version of kind and considerate, and I accepted it. We were different people with very different cleaning techniques.

By Christmastime, I felt a responsibility to go home more than I ever had. It was our first Christmas without my mother, and I wanted it to be as good a celebration as it could be. My mother loved all holidays, especially Christmas. She played Christmas music and decorated the tree with the "adorable" ornaments that my brother and I had made out of tongue depressors and misshapen cotton balls and cardboard squares with our awkward school photos, featuring crooked bangs and a missing tooth. Soon after we grew up and moved out of the house, Ric didn't want a tree, and my mother always compromised by getting a tiny two-foot-tall tree and placing it in the middle of the kitchen table.

This first Christmas without my mother, I lowered my expectations. I traveled home planning on finding an envelope with my name on it, stuffed with the $350 I get every year from Ric. Of course, I always appreciated the cash, but I never understood how he decided upon $350.

Why not $300? And not to be greedy, but why not $500? Nothing happened arbitrarily with Ric. As always, there was some thought, some computation, on his end that was a mystery to me. Assuming he's reading this book, I suppose I could end this mystery by just asking him: Ric, why $350 for Christmas for the past twenty-three years?

It's not an exaggeration to say that when I walked into our home, expecting to find a near-empty house with a couple of envelopes on the kitchen counter, I was astounded to discover that Ric had taken it upon himself to decorate the entire house. There was even a full-size tree in the living room. All of my and my brother's childhood photos on all the Santas' laps were displayed and every ornament was hung on the tree. Like the lively party at our house after my mother's funeral, it was everything my mother had ever wanted, and she wasn't even there to see it.

Being home was suddenly so complicated. I wanted to be surrounded by all the festive decorations my mother would have wanted, but seeing them without her was a little less jolly. When I saw all four of our empty stockings hanging, it was my mother's that made me immediately turn around and walk out of the room, crying with my hands over my face. I sat in my bedroom, wondering what would make me feel better. How could I avoid these emotional land mines? Would it have been any less of a blow if I had walked in and seen just three empty stockings hanging?

Losing a loved one provides a never-ending loop of milestones. There's always the first day, the first week, the first year, the first birthday, the first Mother's Day, the first Christmas; one painful anniversary after another, year after year. And it wasn't just grief that consumed me, but also a feeling of dissociation. There was no place to put "Happy Mother's Day" or "Happy Birthday." The entire "Mother" section of Hallmark cards at the grocery store was no longer talking to me. There was no reason to pick up my phone on days when there used to be. So many things suddenly did not apply to me.

This first year that my mother was gone, Ric began calling nearly every Sunday. It was awkward for me, but it was an awkwardness I was willing to embrace and get used to. I hoped for the day when things between us would become more natural. I hoped that Ric, Renaud, and I would be able to cobble together some semblance of a family. But expecting life to be changed or the past washed away is not realistic. I knew this, but I was able to hope otherwise from a distance until I went home for our second Thanksgiving without my mother and got a sobering reminder that there was still a robot living in the house.

RIC'S HOUSE RULES

Unplug the computer and Internet after each use.

All the food labels in the cabinet must face outward.

Absolutely no letting the car's gas tank get below three-quarters of a tank.

The cat eats only at 6 A.M., noon, and 5 P.M.

No leaving the front door unlocked as you're out getting the mail or waving to a neighbor.

No personal hygiene products left in the bathroom after a visit, not even a sliver of soap.

No food left in the pantry after a visit, even if you are planning on coming back in a month or two.

No leaving the light on in a room, even at night, even if you're just leaving that room—which happens to be your bedroom—for a couple seconds and need the light on so you can see your way back after your relaxing bath.

During that visit, I left my bedroom light on for a moment, and when I returned to the hallway, Ric had shut off my light and stood there in the darkness telling me that anytime I left a room I needed to turn the light off because the bulb would burn out and he could not get up on a ladder to change it. I didn't really care what his reason was. I was rarely home. A light could be on the whole time I was home and not burn out. Even if the bulb did burn out, he could hire a handyman to put in a new one. It occurred to me, and hardly for the first time, that Ric's rules were what mattered most to him, more than the fact that I'm rarely home. In fact, his rules could almost seem designed to keep people away from his home. A heated argument ensued, and I spent the rest of my two days not wanting to leave my room. He had made clear that this was his house, his rules, and that I was merely a visitor who could get the hell out if I had a problem with any of it.

Shortly after my mother died, Ric explained to me that we were no longer legally related. In an effort to make things as clear as possible, he said that since my mother died, we were now as related to each other as we would be to someone off the street. The discussion had come about because my mother's will stated that her belongings—her furniture, etc.—were mine and my brother's. Ric insisted that they all needed to be removed from the house immediately because it was against the law to have them there. As a touring comedian who was, at the time, deathly ill and living in a one-bedroom crash pad, I was not in a position to house furniture that calls for multiple rooms.

Ric's solution: Move it all into a storage unit. I snapped and told Ric to cut me some slack because I was deathly ill. After things cooled down, he decided that he could still follow the rule of law if he bought our mother's belongings from Renaud and me and kept them in the house. Okay, deal, Ric.

Forty-eight hours after the light-bulb incident, I left the house sad and stunned and thoroughly confused. Was Ric just my mother's widower? If we were an actual family, relationships wouldn't be solely defined by contracts. There would have been grace periods for moving furniture, or offers to keep it where it was. There would be compassion. Rules could be broken. What confounds and upsets me the most about Ric is that he seems unwilling or unable to choose his battles or set aside his deep-seated ways and let a light bulb burn for twenty extra seconds or a door be unlocked for one extra minute. Can't a can of V8 juice sit on a shelf until my brother's return or a travel-size shampoo bottle remain in a bathroom that no one ever enters? If Ric wants my brother and me to be closer to him, and I know he does, can't these be the moments when he just takes a beat and reprograms himself? Just a little?

After I left, long silences passed between Ric and me.

I began to fear that after my mother's death, I was just another thing whose function was no longer clear to him, who could be easily thrown way. Four months later, I received a letter from him explaining, in his very pragmatic way, that he didn't always mean things the way they came out, and that he hoped I was doing well, and was sorry that I didn't win the Grammy. The letter touched me deeply. I took it as an apology—his second clear attempt to acknowledge his part in our relationship and to try to make it better—and called him almost immediately. Our phone conversation was our familiar controlled exchange of information:

How are you?

Good.

How's the cat?

She's doing fine.

We are not related, but we are certainly not strangers off the street.

11

Pat

Growing up, I rarely saw my biological father, Pat, which made it easy to plop him on a pedestal, especially when Ric was making me buy back my toys. Certainly, there were a few times when I ran away from Ric, slamming a door and yelling, "I wish my parents never got divorced because Pat would NEVER do this to me!"

Of course, the real reason Pat would never do that to me was because he was almost always missing in action. He and my mother had been partying college kids who popped out a couple of babies and then split.

To this day, my brother and I have probably seen Pat no more than ten times total. Throughout my childhood, he was a mysterious man who would call on the phone for Christmas and birthdays. He never rode my brother and me about our grades or table manners. Our conversations were purely about what fun and exciting things we or he had going on in our lives.

I hardly knew anything about Pat except that he had a mustache. And because of that, I drew mustaches on everything. Even my Snoopy doll received a drawn-on mustache. One weekend, a friend from school had come over to play, and completely out of nowhere as we connected our Lincoln Logs, I said, "My father has a mustache." I cannot explain how much she didn't care. There was no response. I sat there thinking, "Did she not hear me? My father has a mustache! My father has a mustache! I just told her the coolest thing in the world and she didn't even care. Well, I guess that if she didn't care that my father has a mustache, then she's really not going to care that he drives a gutted-out, old van. Fine! I'll keep that one to myself. Her loss."

For years, whenever I passed a man with a mustache driving an old, unmarked van on the highway, I always turned to my girlfriend and said, "There's my father!" (It was kind of like the reverse of the "that's your dad" game.) And it very well could have been my father since he seemed always to be moving around and doing different things. When I was growing up, I remember him being in Jackson, Mississippi; then Denver, Colorado; then

Silver Spring, Maryland. He always had something going on. A job in some town he had to get to, or someone he had to meet up with to concoct some plan that was definitely going to make him money this time. As far as I knew, he mainly worked at motels and pizza parlors or as a security guard.

My brother and I were always excited when my mother sent us to visit with Pat because there was a lot going on. For starters, he wore a holster around his chest with a loaded gun and carried a knife in his cowboy boot. He was always talking to truckers on his CB radio and finding out where the cops were. He gave me the handle "Little Tigger" and I'd tell the truckers, "Breaker one-nine, this is Little Tigger, what's your twenty?" I had no idea I was asking truckers their whereabouts; I just felt like I was right in the middle of some pretty exciting action: guns, CBs, knives, and eighteen-wheelers on the long, straight, desolate highway between Jackson and Hattiesburg. When Pat was the manager of a pizza parlor in Hattiesburg, he drove us to the other pizza joints to check out the competition. Renaud and I sat with him in restaurant parking lots, all of us squeezed in the front bench seat of his early-seventies Oldsmobile Cutlass Supreme, counting other cars. We were on a mission. Pat had guns all over his apartment and a mountain of loose change on top of his only table, a card table that was certainly never dined upon. He brought leftover pizza home from his job and we ate it out of the box. He slept directly on the floor with a single sheet and a pillow. Other kids might have been on summer vacation, but not us. We had things to do before the new school year started. Like politely decline invitations from the next-door neighbor's kids when they asked if we'd like to go squirrel and coon hunting—we had to wait until our father was home from the pizza parlor to be granted permission.

Once when Renaud and I were in Jackson visiting our grandmother Mildred, Pat's mother, he traveled to see us. We were probably around five and six years old, and after spending a couple days with us, he took us both into her garage, squatted down, held one of us in his left arm and the other in his right, and started crying. He explained that he had to go now but wanted us to know how much he loved us, and said to please call him. He began sobbing and said to call him anything. Call him asshole, but just please call him. Anytime. I was scared. I had never seen a grown man cry. I didn't even think men cried, but here was a man with a lot of tears. I thought in that moment that Pat definitely loved us.

Around six months after my mother's death, I heard from my aunt Fran that Pat had been contacting her, distraught over my mother's death and my health.

It had been almost a decade since I had last seen or spoken to him. I had walked offstage after a show in Virginia one night, right past a man standing in the shadows of the back wall, and thought, "Oh, that guy looks like my father." What gave him away was his mustache. I was shocked and flustered. He had driven four hours from Silver Spring, and we sat in the bar eating and talking. Unlike Ric, Pat thought I was a talented, massive celebrity. I was desperate to let him know what level I was really on, that this show was only sold out because it was a holiday show for which businesses would buy discounted tickets for their entire office for a night of "comedy," not a night of Tig. I was pretty confident that no one there even knew who I was before they sat down.

Pat thought I was downplaying my success, and when the manager of the club asked me to sign the club's shot glass for an audience member, it became even more difficult to convince my father that I was no big deal. I was autographing the shot glass with *his* last name. He put me on a pedestal. He confessed to imagining the day he would be interviewed about being Tig Notaro's father. He also wanted to let me know that I could make fun of him in my comedy. Or anywhere. He thought the jokes I made onstage about my mother were funny and said, "Just so you know, I wouldn't care about any jokes you made about me. You can say whatever you want about me." All through my childhood, he had also told me to call the operator and tell them I wanted to make a person-to-person collect call. I still have no idea what the person-to-person part means. These were all nice gestures. On some level, Pat was striving to keep an openness between us.

It also seemed like he was preparing to not see me again for a long time. He told me he'd also purchased tickets to my late show, and I told him I'd be too self-conscious knowing he was in the audience. He graciously agreed not to attend, but it was clear that he had planned on doing anything to see me. He let me know that he took off work for the trip and got a room close to the club so he could walk to the show in case his car broke down. The next day he picked me up and took me to breakfast. He told me I could get whatever I wanted, that it was his treat—as if a couple of scrambled eggs or the Rooty Tooty Fresh 'N Fruity pancakes were an even exchange for being absent all these years. He talked about all his odd jobs and his travels, his general whereabouts after leaving my mother and his infant children, filling in some big, gaping holes I'd always filled in myself. The reality of his life had been nothing I could have imagined. He did this, he did that, and then he had some dealings with the Dixie Mafia in the seventies (at that time, a criminal organization in the South's Gulf Coast region that committed mostly petty crimes). I didn't really understand what I was hearing. Was he a member of the Dixie Mafia? Fighting the Mafia? And if he was fighting the Mafia, why? I know there's always a knife in my father's boot. Even at IHOP. But the more he told me about this Dixie Mafia, the fewer answers I walked away with. All I understood was that the time he spent dealing with the Mafia seemed to be his glory days.

We said good-bye in my hotel parking lot and he started to drive off in something similar to a Cutlass Supreme, then stopped and drove back to me in reverse. He rolled down the window and said he forgot to take some pictures of me and would it be all right if he took some. I said sure, and he snapped photos of me standing awkwardly and alone in the parking lot. When he was finished, he asked me to please get in the car and write a letter to his very young son, my half brother, who I'd never met. He had a notepad and pen ready. So, I sat in a car in the parking lot of a hotel in Virginia writing a letter to my half brother who I'd never met while my father, who I hadn't seen in over ten years, leaned over the center console and watched. After I wrote a vague message that you could give to anybody with working eyeballs, Pat left, satisfied.

The tragedy of my mother's death and my own brushes with death had him reaching out to my aunt. Perhaps he didn't want to intrude too much in my life. Before my world collapsed, I had assumed we had just drifted apart, but now I realized the distance between us had been a long, slow process. How does a father get so far away from his newborn baby? How do you not call your father and tell him your mother died? Would our excuses—moving on, remarrying, I don't have his number, I haven't talked to him in years—sound reasonable to anybody? I'm sure that on his wedding day, or in the hospital when I was being born, it never occurred to my father to imagine a day in the future when he would find out from reading the news that his daughter had cancer or that the woman he married had died in a tragic accident.

I waited almost nine months to e-mail Pat and tell him that I was okay after I heard how upset he was about my mother's death and my health. I felt less pressure to respond right away since he had not contacted me directly, and also because contacting him always stirred up my life, so I had to be certain I was emotionally prepared. At first, I felt like I was essentially writing to a guy who was a fan of mine and bought me breakfast at IHOP once. But as I kept writing, I felt more like I was a child again and writing to the man I thought my father was: a charismatic, loving, funny guy with a mustache; a mysterious and intelligent man who would be the perfect father if only he were there.

Pat's e-mail back was long and full of facts about his life and our family. He was obviously still in pain over the loss of my mother and the news of my health, but I knew that this grief could not kindle any real kind of familial bond between us. I guess I believed there was something inherently broken in Pat's relationship with me and my brother. Maybe we had all missed some ambiguous window of time when we could have salvaged some hope for a real connection. I am certain, however, that we have the same feelings: I want everything to be okay for him and he wants everything to be okay for me.

While writing this book, I heard from my aunt Fran that my father was not doing well.

After years of health problems, he had developed sepsis, a life-threatening complication from an infection. She also informed me that he was showing signs of dementia and it was becoming a struggle for him to talk. The implication was that there was only a very small window of time when I could see him while he was still able to comprehend that I was even there. My aunt and I cried together on the phone, discussing the coulda, shoulda, woulda's. I had not had any communication with Pat since our e-mails about my health, but felt compelled to make an immediate plan to see him. Our clock had run out, and I was feeling a complicated mix of anger and sadness. As a parent, hadn't he had the foresight to see that this was the position that we would ultimately end up being in? The position of having to say good-bye when we barely had anything to say good-bye to? I only had a few scattered real memories of Pat among the thousands I should have had. There was no life he was living for me other than the glimpses I had caught of him: eating pizza and trying to get the highest score on Asteroids or Pac-Man; walking into public establishments with a loaded gun strapped across his chest; reaching into his back pocket and pulling out a generic black comb and brushing his mustache while chewing on a toothpick.

Several weeks after Fran called, we traveled to Silver Spring together. I had a return ticket for the following day, figuring a short visit would be best, as I expected things to be intense since I was not only saying good-bye to my father, but meeting his wife and my half brother for the very first time. When we pulled into his apartment complex, I steered us straight toward an old blue van and parked, knowing I must be close. Sure enough, about ten yards away, there was my father, alone and pacing back and forth, looking around nervously. From a distance, he almost reminded me of a lost puppy.

Fran and I walked up to him, then each of us hugged him. He was so frail and anxious, standing there in front of the glass door to the apartment building. For all I knew, he'd been standing there all morning, waiting and pacing. He reached out to hug me, with an emotional and stuttered "I love you." I had been unable to imagine the effects of his dementia until now. It was heartbreaking to hear him try to speak. My mother's dementia hadn't been as obvious. You would only catch her slipping up if you had any depth of a relationship with her; otherwise she could pretty easily blend in with life. Pat, on the other hand, was barely hanging on to life.

We followed him into a small one-bedroom apartment with very minimal belongings. He proudly introduced me to Susan, a very sweet-natured and pretty Filipina who nodded and welcomed me in broken English. And then there was Anthony. We didn't need a formal introduction. It was clear who the other one was. He had those dimples Pat had so generously doled out to all his children. I was blown away by how handsome he was, how sincere. I'd heard he was a competitive break dancer, which was a subject I knew nothing about, but I was very intrigued. He was nineteen and going on forty with all the responsibility I'd heard he'd taken on since our father had gotten sick—bathing Pat and driving him to all his doctor appointments while working a full-time job doing maintenance at the local mall so he could help support the family. Anthony hugged me so intensely and warmly—he certainly wasn't some awkward or distant guy acting too cool to meet his long-lost sister. He was beaming with excitement, so eager to know me. Even though I'd come here to let go of something, I saw very clearly that I was also gaining something amazing.

We all pulled different types of chairs together from different parts of the room, making sort of a wobbly half circle, and took each other in, passing smiles back and forth. With my father's struggle to speak, Susan's lack of

English, and my cautious entrance into their world, we were hardly catching up, but timidly stepping into an introduction. Fran officially began things by asking me to tell everyone about how they could see me on TV the following evening. "I am going to be a guest on *The Late Late Show* tomorrow, Wednesday," I said slowly, so that my father could understand, so that Susan could understand, and so I could gauge the temperature of the room. Susan acknowledged my news with a supportive smile and my brother was completely giddy, full of questions about Hollywood and being a comedian, and thrilled to report how he tells people that I'm his sister.

"All the blessings in the world to you," my father said. "All the blessings in the world."

The conversation flowed more easily from there, most of it happening between Anthony, Fran, and me, with my father chiming in when he could. I always feel very lucky and aware of Fran's constant support, but I felt especially aware and lucky on this particular afternoon. When we were leaving, I asked my father, who had been sitting on a very worn, low-quality office chair, if he possibly wanted a new one, suggesting that he might be more comfortable in a big recliner that I would be happy to order for him. He affectionately tapped his hand on the chair's plastic arm, explaining that he'd had it forever, to which I replied, "Yes, that's very apparent." Everyone laughed with us.

I know what it felt like for me, but I can't help but wonder what it felt like for a parent to be waving good-bye to their child for the very last time.

Seven months later, after shooting a TV show in Mississippi centering mostly around my mother's death, I landed back in Los Angeles and turned on my cell phone to discover that sometime when I was in midair, my father had passed away. Every day since I had left Pat's apartment, I had been expecting the call that I had just missed. I was seated next to our show's costume designer and the actor who plays my brother. I fought back tears while waiting for everyone to deplane or whatever that stupid word is that's now popular to describe exiting an aircraft. Despite the kindness of my coworkers, I felt immensely trapped and crowded out of my ability to grieve alone.

As soon as we got close to baggage claim, we were swiftly ushered by police, or military personnel, holding serious-looking rifles to an area between a wall and a carousel and ordered to get down and stay away from the doors and glass. There had been a credible bomb threat to LAX.

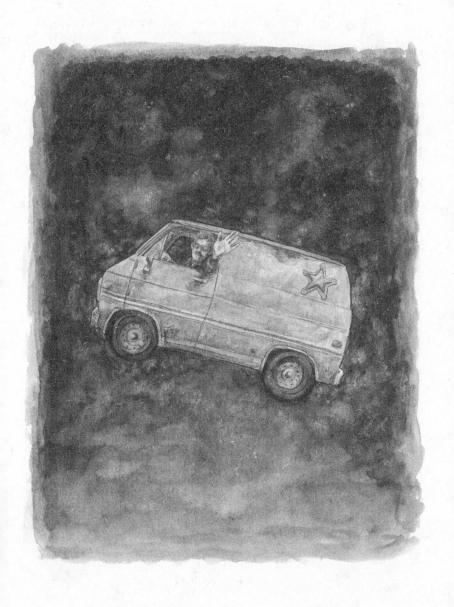

I got low and hid with the other travelers, where my intermittent crying blended right in with everyone crouched around me also crying. More and more military personnel began lining the area around us, and people started frantically dialing loved ones. I heard voices saying, "Dad?" . . . "Honey—it's Mom." I was scared. I tried making a few phone calls but could not get anyone to answer.

12

Stage IV

On March 1 of 2013, it had been a year since I got the tickle in my throat—the beginning of my life's unraveling. Shortly after that, I had been bedridden with a severe sinus infection and bronchitis that turned into pneumonia. Then: one year since I had collapsed and gone to the emergency room, was admitted to the hospital, and was diagnosed with C-diff; one year since I got the call that my mother had an accidental fall and wasn't going to make it; one year since I took her off life support. When my birthday, March 24, rolled around, it felt more than ever like the anniversary of surviving.

Thinking I was being thorough, I made a checkup appointment with a new oncologist (my original doctor had gotten married and moved to San Diego six months earlier, right before my surgery). My new oncologist was in total disbelief that I had let six months pass between my surgery and a follow-up. She wanted to start me on hormone blockers immediately, explaining that I should have been on them soon after surgery and that my risk for recurrence was much higher if I wasn't taking them.

She then told me something I didn't remember hearing before: Because I had gotten rid of all my breast tissue, if there were any cancer cells that had been missed in surgery, they would return to places such as bones, lungs, and blood. At that point, the cancer would no longer be stage II. It would be stage IV and incurable. I was told that if I went on hormone blockers right then, my chance of recurrence would be 7 percent.

The fact that I took in any information at all is nothing short of unbelievable. Being diagnosed with cancer was a full-time job with plenty of overtime. It felt like being teleported directly into medical school from the eighth-grade science class that I failed. Doctors may very well have told me I needed to start hormone blockers right after surgery, or to come back every three months to have "levels" checked, but I didn't hear it. I only recall my doctors suggesting precautionary chemotherapy following surgery, which I had decided against because it would be brutal on my system, which was still recovering from C-diff, and would make my chances for getting pregnant in the future slim to none.

Five months before my diagnosis, when I felt as healthy as I'd ever been, I had been actively moving toward getting pregnant. I focused my vision on being a mother and making the blob more of a concretely formed tiny person. I was talking with doctors and potential male donors and had visions of touring with a baby and having my opening act be lucky enough to babysit in the greenroom backstage. Then I was diagnosed and told that my kind of breast cancer was fed by hormones and that if I had gotten pregnant, as I'd hoped, the nine-month spike in hormones would have likely killed me. Carrying a child of my own was now completely off the table.

My new oncologist explained that even harvesting my eggs for IVF would be like "throwing gas on a fire" since it would also increase my hormone levels, and she was adamant about me starting the hormone blockers immediately. This left me at the crossroads of one of the most difficult decisions of my life.

After two weeks of exhausting deliberation, and encouraged by my surgeon's belief that she had gotten it all, I decided to harvest my eggs for IVF, which meant delaying the hormone blockers even longer.

As complicated and irresponsible as it sounds, I felt certain that I would regret it for the rest of my life if I did not risk my own life in trying to have a child. And if trying to have a child caused my cancer to come back, then, I reasoned, the regret would most likely be very short-lived. Again, probably not very sound reasoning, but I was shell-shocked by the gravity of my few options and stunned by the thought "This isn't how my life is supposed to go."

My fertility doctor and oncologist had devised a plan they determined to be the least life-threatening: I would take one round of hormone treatments in order to optimize the number of eggs available for harvesting, then I would immediately start taking hormone blockers. It took nearly six months to research and organize the IVF and surrogate processes, and each day I imagined my 7 percent chance of having a terminal cancer diagnosis rapidly growing in the wrong direction. I pictured cancer cells returning as little black dots scattered throughout my body. When I finally began injecting myself with the fertility hormones, I pretty much saw fire racing down a trail of gasoline.

Besides the unpleasantness of envisioning shooting myself up with what was essentially terminal cancer fuel, the injections were extremely painful. I had to put a two-inch needle into my thigh and stomach twice a day for eight days. My body became sorer and sorer, and along with the risk of my cancer returning as stage IV, there were some side effects I had to deal with: depression, headaches, vomiting, stomach pain, and nausea (yes, all of these, please), diarrhea (sure, why stop there?), breast enlargement (worth a shot), and freckles. (Please, God, not freckles—I don't deserve that. Haven't I been through enough?)

To face these risks, I clearly had to be somebody who really wanted kids. At the end of my eight days of injections, I experienced one of the side effects: a nose dive into depression. It only lasted twenty-four hours, but it was the darkest time in my life; a day and a night in which I had no hope and happened to be booked to do a show in St. Paul, Minnesota.

In my late teens and part of my twenties, I had been diagnosed with depression, but it was so far in the past I had forgotten its debilitating intensity. During my ride from my hotel to the beautiful, old theater where the show would take place, I felt completely devoid of appetite, interest, or care for anything, really. Talking to my driver or anyone, even having to share the same space with another person, was beyond exhausting. I sat alone in the greenroom, staring at a few bottles of water in front of me, waiting to hear my name announced, and trying to endure an unbearable sense of heaviness and nothingness. In twenty minutes, I had to go onstage before roughly a thousand people, and I felt like I was on a ledge. I pictured it as the edge of a tall building—not one I wanted to jump off of, but one I could not step away from. I was incapable of going forward or backward. I didn't care about the audience filing into the theater. I didn't care about anything. I called my friend Stef, who told me to keep reminding myself that this was the hormone treatment, that it was only temporary, and that it would go away.

Intellectually, I knew she was right: I had, hours before, injected the very hormones that were causing this feeling of NO RETURN, but I could not convince myself that I would ever be okay again. I was certain I had a terrible life and had nothing to look forward to. Waiting behind the curtain, I felt eerily similar to how I felt behind the curtain during the Largo show, just a year before. I was waiting in a very dark place, about to have to go make other people smile, laugh, and forget their problems. Only this time, somehow, it felt so much bleaker. I didn't even have the nervousness that had helped propel me onto the stage at Largo. When I heard my name called, I audibly sighed, and walked toward the curtain, thinking, "Okay, here we go . . ."

I could not believe where I was by the time I walked offstage. It was as though I had entered a time capsule and traveled back to the elated, on-top-of-the world, at-my-best self that I usually am after a show. I don't always have a good show and feel wonderful, but doing a live performance is often very therapeutic. I lift the audience; they lift me. There have been times I've gone onstage with crippling stomach pains, on the day of a breakup, and moments after finding out a friend died, and each time I stepped off of the stage feeling stronger, better, and more equipped to face life. After St. Paul, I was on high alert for signs that I could swing back into that hor-rifically dark place, but thankfully, I had finished the last several days of hormone injections without feeling any-thing worse than the pain of the needle.

Of the nine eggs that were extracted, only one be-came a viable embryo. The doctors were very clear that any more harvesting of eggs was not an option if I wanted to maintain my chances of survival. This embryo would be my only shot using my own eggs. I named him Jack.

I tried to plan for having the baby and then possibly

being told I had terminal cancer. Essentially, it was a time of planning my baby shower and my own funeral. One day, when I was sick with the repercussions of C-diff, I made a rough draft of my will on the back of a grocery list. Either side of the paper would have believably been my will. For instance: *Bananas*.

I continued to struggle to believe that it wasn't all a horrible thing to do: having a child while knowing I might not be around to raise it, and that possibly my not being around to raise it was because I chose to harvest my eggs in the first place. I felt selfish, but I didn't know how not to be. Having a kid was something I felt almost crazily okay with being selfish about. Motherhood was a far more tangible direction to head than gloom. Thinking about a kid was a way to have something to continue to live for.

I called my childhood friend Meggan, who was aware of my diagnosis but didn't know all the details of my fertility travails. I knew in my heart that she would be a wonderful mother and wouldn't hesitate to raise my child alongside her own children. Although clearly sad to be having the conversation, Meggan was touched and insistent that she and her husband would be honored to raise my child. Whatever was coming my way, I felt a huge sense of security and happiness knowing I had made the best possible decision about Jack's future on the heels of possibly one of the worst decisions I'd ever made.

Like my cancer diagnosis, I flip-flopped between excitement and hope, and fear and dread. I pictured all the different ways my hip downtown L.A. loft would become one big nursery. I would make sure to have a crib on wheels so I could roll it from my bedroom into the main room. A little soft teddy bear would be lying on the couch; a pacifier would be on the kitchen counter between a baby bottle and a dirty coffee cup. I've always wanted to raise a child who could be comfortable anywhere, even in the middle of chaos, and for years had imagined plopping my sleeping child down on a bed of coats at a friend's dinner party or imagining us fearlessly riding atop an elephant. I don't know why I always pictured riding an elephant with my kid, maybe it symbolized going to the ends of the earth together and experiencing something bigger and greater.

The fertility doctor told me the chances Jack would "take" in the surrogate were low, about 14 percent, and that we would know in a couple weeks. How was it that all extremely pertinent information about my life was being presented in percentages now? I tried to stay positive as my brain bounced around with its limited comprehension of what these numbers actually meant. One of the only things I knew for sure was that seven was half of fourteen. So, by those calculations, if the chances for the baby's life were deemed very low, then maybe this meant my chances of getting a terminal cancer diagnosis were not as frightening. The other side of the percentage finally started to occur to me. I had a 93 percent chance of living—which frankly is probably higher than what I had all along in life.

My 93 percent chance at life, however, hinged on me taking those hormone blockers as soon as I completed my egg retrieval. The list of possible side effects of taking the blockers was just as terrifying as the consequences of not taking them: blood clots in lungs and legs, stroke, endometrial and uterine cancers, depression, hot flashes, and bloating. I delayed taking them for another couple months until it sank into my brain that cancer recurrence was my biggest threat and a far more tangible one than the side effects of the medication (of which, I've only suffered hot flashes and good old-fashioned bloating).

Those little blacks dots continued to rear their imaginary heads but were beginning to carry less and less weight. There was no Mary Tyler Moore awakening, just the realization that everyone has an "end day" coming, and that I was no different. I could sit around moping about my death while a friend, who spent no time moping about hers, could be hit by that ever-popular, ever-reckless bus that seems to run over everyone's friend or loved one whenever they're brought up in any hypothetical scenario.

There's a long list of amazing people I've dated. Gorgeous, intelligent, hilarious, successful, kind, talented, wackadoodle. You name it, I've dated it. Yet, somehow, I had never been in a relationship with a person I truly saw a future with. I always thought, "Huh, I wonder when this will end?" I wondered what was wrong with me that I dated so many people but couldn't find someone I was sure about. I tried desperately to ignore these thoughts and just be in the relationship, but there was always an excuse: They smoke, they're in debt, I don't fit in with their friends and family, they drink too much, they eat gross food, they're too sensitive and needy, we don't live in the same city, they have no direction, they're obsessed with social media and TV, they're too young, they're too old, they don't want kids, they want to move in, they're smothering, they want marriage too desperately. Although these were all valid reasons for a relationship not to work, they were only half the reason. I was the other half. I travel too much, I can be emotionally distant, I hate small talk and am not tremendous in social situations, I'm more uptight about excessive drinking than most, I have germ issues, I can be very particular in my ways and am not so easygoing with restaurant choices, I hate crowds and loud anything, I cannot fake laugh for you, and unfortunately, I don't enjoy your dog jumping all over me, I wish I did, but I really just don't. Trust me, the list goes on.

Whenever I met a couple who seemed genuinely connected, I had a million questions for them. "How did you meet? How long have you been together? When did you know? How did you know?" Every time I dated someone, there was always someone sitting in the next rotating seat. I hated this part of my life.

Along came Stephanie. I ran into her in January of 2013, days after returning from New York, and right before I learned that added to the list of my own inadequacies would be incurable cancer, should it return. I was in the greenroom at the UCB Theatre in Los Angeles, and she walked up and said hello. We'd technically met nine months earlier, just before I was hospitalized for C-diff, when she played my love interest in my friend Lake Bell's movie *In a World*, but I was in a relationship with Brooke and so sick that I hadn't seen Stephanie as a romantic option. I only remembered liking her a lot and really enjoying our exchanges while on set. At the UCB Theatre, however, she lit up to me. I loved her cool, classic style and beauty. All of our great conversations and belly laughs on the set of *In a World* came rushing back to me.

A week later, I was pretty suspicious about our behavior. We had both gone from devout nontexters to people with full-blown technological addictions. Day and night, we were keeping one another abreast of any fleeting thoughts. I was still casually seeing Jessie, but it was becoming obvious that our relationship had no future. More than ever, I wanted stability, and there was nothing stable about our relationship. Also, Jessie had admitted that she had issues with dishonesty and was trying very hard to practice honesty, but she seemed to only do it in moments that were easy. For instance, there were several nights we were together when she showed me texts she'd just received from a comedian I considered to be a good friend, who played drums in a very short-lived band with Jessie and me, and knew we were involved. She'd say, "Hey your drummer is asking me out again. What should I do?" In these moments, I thought she was being very open with me. Later, I realized she was telling me she had no interest in this person, so there really was nothing at stake for her, despite the air of intimate honesty.

I had mostly shrugged this issue off because I didn't feel we were moving toward a real future, but it turns out honesty is important, whether it's with a stranger on the street or with someone in a temporary relationship. The split was surprisingly hard on both of us, but I never regretted being with her. Our being together made perfect sense when it first began, when I needed a wild distraction. Now the last thing I wanted was to be distracted. I wanted to be keenly aware and open to all the possibilities in my 93 percent shot at life.

There was something very available about Stephanie. She wasn't wild; she was calm and thoughtful. She was one of the most transparent people I'd ever met. Fairly quickly, I knew that whatever she told me was how she felt and there'd be no curve-ball follow-up or mixed message. Something else about her attracted me very deeply, something that made her different from other people. For several months, I tried to name this quality until, finally, I realized that one of the most overwhelming feelings I had for her was respect. I'd had respect for previous girlfriends, but it was more along the lines of a general appreciation for who they were. But one morning, as I watched Stephanie get ready for the day, it hit me that the high level of respect I had for her simply came out of the undeniable respect she had for herself.

"Oh my gosh," I said while she got dressed. "I just realized what that thing is about you that's been driving me crazy. I have never heard you say one negative thing about yourself. Not even in self-deprecation." She replied that she never would, even though she knew she had plenty of room for self-improvement. My head exploded. I had never been with someone who didn't express self-doubt or wasn't hard on themselves in some way. To be with someone so self-possessed leaves so much more room for quality time together. No one needs to be knocked down just to be built up again, or built up just to be knocked down. There are no fights about someone saying the wrong thing or needing reassurance about how they look, who they are, or where they are in life. When I marveled over our compatibility and how easy things were with us, she said she just believed that it was true that I loved and cared for her, and she tried always to assume that nothing I said or did was intentionally done to hurt her. My head exploded again. These were reasonable thoughts, ones I identified with, but I had never heard them expressed so succinctly. I certainly had never seen them in action to this degree.

Yes, she *was* the next girl in the rotating seat, but she was very different. But I was very different, too. To some degree, I had been wound up and unavailable my whole life, until my repeated encounters with death. My horrible year loosened a thread in me, Stephanie pulled it, and I unraveled. I felt comfortable and safe with her. Not one single thing about her bugged me. Even when she opened her astrology and dream interpretation books and wanted to have a discussion about her findings—an activity that would normally send me running—I was genuinely interested in her interpretations. If Stephanie was interested, I was interested. I had never felt so open to anyone.

Stephanie and I had only been dating a month when I had dinner with our mutual friend Robbie. He referred to Stephanie as "the marrying type." I'd never really considered marriage, but when he said this, I took a beat and realized, "Yeah, I guess she is the marrying type." And then, "Here I am dating the marrying type." A seed was planted, and in the second month of dating Stephanie, I found myself—me, the person who got uptight when a girlfriend decided it was time to leave her toothbrush

at my house—sitting across the table from her at a restaurant and compelled to say, "I have something really
crazy to tell you. I feel like I want to get married to you."
As if I'd mentioned that the restaurant should turn down
the air-conditioning, she very casually responded with
"Yeah, that's how I feel." I was expecting a more shocked
response from her, like that I needed to relax and let
things breathe a bit.

It felt crazy that we both felt so strongly about our future together. We pictured where our wedding might be
and how our barefoot kids would run through our backyard, past our organic vegetable garden. We both saw our
cat, Fluff, who probably wasn't even a twinkle in some
other kitty's eye, lounging in a patch of sun beneath our
window.

It's rare enough to want the same things as anyone
else, let alone at the same time, and then tack on a fifteen-
year age difference. If before, friends had called many
of my happenstances "Tig Luck," what could I call my
situation now? Anytime I began to believe I was lucky, I
was immediately reminded of the series of very unlucky
events that I'd just narrowly survived, and knew that,
technically, I was probably not what you would call lucky.
But it sure felt right to call myself the luckiest unlucky

person alive. Or maybe it was more appropriate and rational to just say that extraordinary things were happening, both good and bad, and, really, they always had.

Six months into dating, Stephanie moved herself and towers of books and pressed button-down, collared shirts into my loft. The grainy black-and-white ultrasound photo of the dot that was Jack was still on the fridge. Two and a half months earlier, I'd learned that he did not make it. I was grateful not to be carrying this sorrow on my own. Stephanie had gotten me excited about the 14 percent chance of Jack's survival—she'd believed it was somehow in my favor that the odds were so low since I'd been someone beating the odds my whole life. At first, trying to build a family after losing the possibility of Jack felt like forcing myself to keep pushing through with the knowledge that my next possible disappointment was waiting around the corner, but Stephanie's infectious positivity replaced my dread and fear with hope and excitement. When we first met, I didn't relate to her goal of wanting to live to be a hundred years old. I always thought making it to seventy would be a reasonable amount of time to be kicking around. But after we'd committed to one another, she was very vocal about wanting us to die around the same time. Anytime I told her that was impossible, she encouraged me with "You can do it!" as if it were my choice. I usually replied, "I'm so sorry, but with our age difference and my health issues, you're going to die alone—it's just for sure." As we grew closer and more happy than I ever imagined I could be with someone, I shockingly found myself fantasizing about living to a hundred and fifteen, like she was pressuring me to do.

As I finish this book, Stephanie just turned thirty and I'll reach the ripe, young age of forty-five in March. We ended up getting married in my hometown of Pass Christian, where my mother and Ric also married. I never wanted marriage for myself, but I didn't know how not to be married to Stephanie, just like I didn't know how not to fall in love with her or move in together. I knew our wedding would be an amazing time, but I had no earthly idea that it would be the absolute best time of my life. Each face in the crowd was one of our favorite people in the world, celebrating our love in this small Mississippi town. It was a very quiet sadness not to see my mother in that crowd, but it was joyous to see Ric beaming with so much pride and love. I've always known he wanted the best for me, but now he was actively showing it. He told Stephanie and me that he wanted to make sure we had the exact wedding that we imagined. Not only did Ric end up paying for our stunning, storybook ceremony and using his legal expertise to sort out the contracts with vendors, he began stepping out of the background in other ways to fulfill the role of "parents" (which I still had programmed in my cell phone as his contact name). Of course, the days of "ask your mother" were gone, but slowly and surely, so were the days of "too bad" and "I have no sympathy for you." He even suggested that Stephanie and I join him and Renaud on a trip to Europe in the near future— this coming from the same man who had to essentially be forced to take the two family vacations we took in a forty-two-year span of time.

Part of wanting to be keenly aware and available to all the possibilities in my life is learning when to say no. I've worked hard and have been lucky enough to always be moving onward and upward in my comedy career. For the first fourteen years, I spent two to three weeks a month on the road, going from city to city, country to country. When I wasn't traveling, I was performing five to seven nights a week in Los Angeles. The only real stall-out was the four months when my life fell apart.

Having spent most of that year in and out of the hospital, fearful that I was close to my deathbed, I naturally came across people who were close to dying themselves. Who cares that it's cliché, this was their one common regret: They wished they had worked less and spent more time with their loved ones. I pride myself on living with no regrets, and I certainly don't want any in my final moments. I've always tried to be aware of an opportunity to change something I might later regret. I quit smoking when I was twenty-five because I didn't want to be one of those people who is fifty and wishing they had quit when they were twenty-five. This last year was one big moment in which I realized that I was no longer interested in making every appearance on every live performance, or having my face pop up on any random TV show I'm offered. I want to have faith that I can make a decent living without devoting all of my time to my career. I want to be more deliberate with the choices I make and the people I surround myself with. I've achieved a balance that didn't seem possible before: a successful career with a loving and promising home life and more time off to spend with family and friends.

I also have a 7 percent chance of imminent, early death, and not a day goes by that I am unaware of this.

The slightest pain or inflammation is still a startling discovery that sends me flying down the road to urgent care. For several days, I had a dull ache in my hip that became sharp when I stood up or moved in a particular way. One Google led to another, and pretty soon I was certain I would have the same fate as John Edwards's late wife, Elizabeth—a breast cancer survivor who later died of bone cancer, which first announced itself with pain in her hip. The next morning, Stephanie and I drove to the doctor in near silence. After an examination, the doctor told me I had some inflammation in my hip and that he'd be back shortly with a prescription for anti-inflammatories. The moment he left the room, Stephanie and I promptly began hugging and crying on each other's shoulder like we'd both just heard that I was going to live. Which, basically, we had. When the doctor returned, I asked if this was the most dramatic response he'd gotten to diagnosing inflammation of the hip. He laughed awkwardly as we choked on our tears and continued embracing each other.

It's not easy to keep moving forward with a positive outlook. I have the sense that I'm teetering on a very thin line. When I take my pills in the morning, I imagine them working toward ensuring the 93 percent chance at life that I have. When I eat ice cream or a piece of birthday cake, I remember the 7 percent and picture the tiny granules of sugar dispersing into some vulnerable area of my body, feeding any possible lingering, hungry cancer cells the surgeon missed. To an outsider, 7 percent might seem like a great prognosis. Tig, why are you even going into this? This is great news! And it *is* great news and a great prognosis. But when it's your prognosis, you never forget the 7 percent. You just keep going.

The scary beauty of life is that cancer can be around the corner just as a Grammy nomination can be. People ask all the time if I'm mad that it took cancer to get me the recognition that I deserved. I tell them no, that I'm perfectly happy with how everything has unfolded in my life. Cancer didn't propel me. It's what I did with my cancer diagnosis that propelled me. There were many moments when I felt too depressed to go anywhere, and sitting on my couch and having cancer seemed like the only thing I could do. I was trapped in a dark, narrow space where only two thoughts took turns in my mind: "If I have very little time left, I should do everything in the world that I can possibly do." And then, "Why bother? If I have very little time left, would anything I do make a difference to me or anyone? Why not just let cancer take me?"

When I was first diagnosed I did sit on my couch having cancer—for a little over a week—until I felt unable to do it anymore. That felt like giving up, giving in, and essentially dying. So when Flanagan asked me if I was still going to do my Largo show, I knew I had to. If I was dying, this was going to be the moment that would make me feel most alive.

I am so thankful I got off the couch and found that audience. During the course of my comedy career, I've often had ideas that weren't quite my style, and I told myself no, you're not a physical comedian; no, you're not a storyteller; no, you don't use props; no, you don't share personal details. Yet I tried every one of these things and they pushed me to new levels and brought me successes I never would have reached had I stayed comfortably within the narrow confines of who I thought I was. I cannot express how important it is to believe that taking one tiny—and possibly very uncomfortable—step at a time can ultimately add up to a great distance.

The other scary beauty of life, which I probably should have expected to discover in all of this, was how heightened circumstances, such as overlapping tragedy and success, sharpen your vision and shorten your patience for baloney and hogwash.

It seems that for some people, there are more convenient times to be there and less convenient times to be there. The complicated dynamic that comes with simultaneous hopeless and successful circumstances can kick up jealousy, misunderstanding, unrealistic expectations, dishonesty, fear, rage, and all sorts of other unfortunate realities. These past couple years, there have been friends and celebrated people who I came to discover were ruthless and inappropriate, and whose aims and goals clashed terribly with my own. I want success and happiness but not at any cost.

Through all this, I learned that I'm a really bad match for certain people, and that, although we might forever be tied to each other in the eyes of the public, it was totally okay to dissociate myself from them in my personal life. I wanted to put my time and energy toward mutually fulfilling, nurturing, and growing relationships. Health and peace of mind override everything.

My mother and Pat both had passions and a certain sense of personal freedom, but I think they were both confined by some misguided notions about what they could and couldn't do and never realized their full potential. Pat could build and program computers, and I'd suggested several times that he try to make a career in computers.

His response was always "You don't turn your hobby into your job." I could not disagree more. My mother, on the other hand, could have thrived almost anywhere in the arts—painting, comedy, dancing. She also loved getting a reaction. I can imagine a couple gasps, a few "O lordy's" and "Heavens to Betsy's," and an "Oh, my, my" on the night of the party for her engagement to my father, when she celebrated a toast by Pat's side of the family—all of whom she'd just met—by throwing her wineglass across the room, where it smashed against the brick wall of Great-Aunt Mellie's farmhouse. She continued to shock and entertain the family, but the spark in her suggested she probably would have appreciated a larger audience.

I read a quote once that really resonated with me, and I made little changes to it so that it could apply more directly to my life: "The best gift you can give anyone is a well-lived life of your own." Had my parents done this, I think that the weight of my worry and concern for their happiness and well-being would have been lifted.

After my life changed, the press portrayed my relationship with my mother as nothing short of harmonious. I tried to be fair about our relationship without derailing an interview with too many details about our complex dynamic, but there was so much good about my mother that it was hard not to feed into the press's image. And in truth, the only nice part about her death is that my memories have been set to a default mode that mainly pulls up her highlight reel. It's not that I now have a false sense of who she was; it's just that she was my mother, my original temple. My first hero. My source of life.

My mother being the exception, it was hard to realize I had no control over how the press was going to handle all the other details of my life. It continues to drive me insane that it keeps being reported that my girlfriend left me when I got diagnosed with cancer. For the record: This is not the case in the slightest. Brooke and I had mutually broken up weeks before. And for the record: With time and peace to reflect, I realized that if it weren't for Brooke—who insisted that I get my lumps checked out—I never would have mentioned anything to the doctor after my C-diff follow-up examination. I probably would have answered her, "Was there anything else?" with "No." And then, very soon, there might not have been anything else.

These days, I am very easily one of the happiest people you could cross paths with. I am surrounded by the most loving friends and family, and the life Stephanie and

I have begun to build with our kitten, Fluff, is beyond anything I had ever imagined for myself.

My mother always said: "Life is all about change, and if you can't keep up with it, it's going to leave you behind." Her words have guided me through C-diff, breast cancer, and ultimately, through the loss of her. Now her words have helped allow me to discover that I do want marriage for myself, and that I'm fully committed to building a history with someone as we negotiate our way through life, grow old together, and hopefully die well into our hundreds at the exact same time, buried side by side in that plot Ric scored such a sweet deal on.

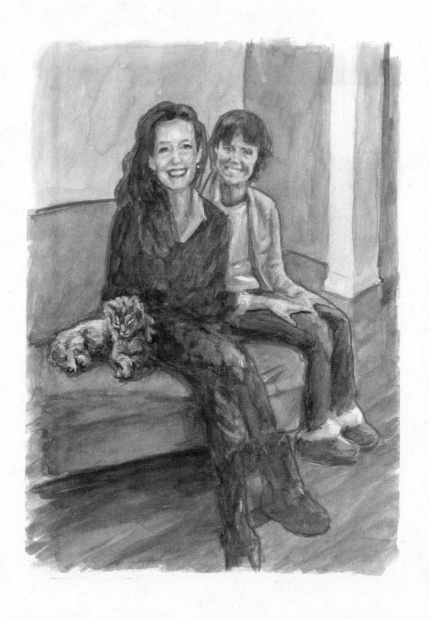